T0311351

Law, Space, and the Vehicular Environment

This book examines the paved road as a liminal space and legal frontier for enlivened, everyday struggles over property, power, and place/definition. Through pavement itself and the pavement-based practices of pavementalities and pavementeering, the road is legally framed as a place for movement.

Paved terrain is a site of dynamism between law and place that engenders the road as legal metaphor by calling forth the kinetic notion of jurisprudence in which law can be understood through the fluidity of everyday life. In Western (and particularly American) society, roads are a material locus of governance, in which rights of way are determined, communicated, and enforced. However, roads also constitute a site of resistance or disruption, beyond regulation. Addressing phenomena such as travel, political protest, public memory, and community governance, this book explores the paved medium of asphalt as a complex surface for legality that constitutively frames order against disorder involving jurisdiction tensions, property ownership, and cultural identities in vehicular environments.

The target audience of this book are those students and scholars who consider how law works in society, whether through frameworks of (auto) mobility and legal geography or through the interdisciplinary approaches of legal semiotics, legal culture, and/or new materialism.

Sarah Marusek is Professor of Public Law in the Political Science Department at the University of Hawai'i Hilo, USA.

Space, Materiality and the Normative

Series Editors: Andreas Philippopoulos-Mihalopoulos and Christian Borch

Space, Materiality and the Normative presents new ways of thinking about the connections between space and materiality from a normative perspective. At the interface of law, social theory, politics, architecture, geography and urban studies, the series is concerned with addressing the use, regulation and experience of space and materiality, broadly understood, and in particular with exploring their links and the challenges they raise for law, politics and normativity.

Law, Space, and the Vehicular Environment
Pavement and Asphalt
Sarah Marusek

www.routledge.com/Space-Materiality-and-the-Normative/book-series/ SMNORM

Law, Space, and the Vehicular Environment

Pavement and Asphalt

Sarah Marusek

Routledge
Taylor & Francis Group
a GlassHouse Book

First published 2023
by Routledge
4 Park Square, Milton Park, Abingdon, Oxon OX14 4RN

and by Routledge
605 Third Avenue, New York, NY 10158

Routledge is an imprint of the Taylor & Francis Group, an informa business

A GlassHouse book

© 2023 Sarah Marusek

The right of Sarah Marusek to be identified as author of this work has been asserted in accordance with sections 77 and 78 of the Copyright, Designs and Patents Act 1988.

British Library Cataloguing-in-Publication Data
A catalogue record for this book is available from the British Library

Library of Congress Cataloging-in-Publication Data
Names: Marusek, Sarah, author.
Title: Law, space, and the vehicular environment : pavement and asphalt / Sarah Marusek.
Description: Abingdon, Oxon ; New York, NY : Routledge, 2023. | Series: Space, materiality and the normative | Includes bibliographical references and index.
Identifiers: LCCN 2022031610 (print) | LCCN 2022031611 (ebook) | ISBN 9781138293823 (hardback) | ISBN 9781032407555 (paperback) | ISBN 9781315231853 (ebook)
Subjects: LCSH: Space in economics. | Roads.
Classification: LCC HT388 .M37 2023 (print) | LCC HT388 (ebook) | DDC 388.1—dc23/eng/20220804
LC record available at https://lccn.loc.gov/2022031610
LC ebook record available at https://lccn.loc.gov/2022031611

ISBN: 978-1-138-29382-3 (hbk)
ISBN: 978-1-032-40755-5 (pbk)
ISBN: 978-1-315-23185-3 (ebk)

DOI: 10.4324/9781315231853

Typeset in Times New Roman
by Apex CoVantage, LLC

Contents

Figures

Preface

I've been fascinated by the pavement for a long time. Nearly every time I climb in the front seat of a car I wonder, what is so compelling about a yellow line in the middle and a white line on the edge to make cars nearly always drive between them? Why do we drive between these painted lines? Why do we prefer, if not simply expect, to drive our cars on smooth asphalt rather than a rough, crumbling graveled surface? Clearly, the reasoning may be self-serving, as we don't want to hit another car in crossing the yellow line or bung up our automobile from driving on rocks or over holes. However, it may also be in the interest of others, as we don't want to mow down a pedestrian who may be walking on the white line of the road's shoulder or another car coming towards on the other side of the yellow line. It may even be that we fear the negative response of law enforcement, who may ticket our rebellious or inattentive driving. With these things in mind, I think it's much more. In fact, I'm pretty sure that the role that asphalt plays in our vehicularized lives is much more than just a smooth surface for driving. As I assert in this book, pavement itself is a source of law and legality in which the dimensionality of the surface of the road and the tensions that dimensionality fosters and sustains lead us to consider the road as a place and a site of legal geography. As the site for automobility, the road itself begets and engenders the myriad interactions between drivers within the atmosphere of pavement. This asphalted roadscape is a place in which governance, compliance, and resistance enliven the understandings and practices of law that we routinely perpetuate, yet challenge every time we drive down the road. As a site of legal geography that is rife with legal semiotics, spatial politics, and cultural jurisdictional engagement, the roadscape plays a vital yet underexamined platform for seeing how we navigate, dwell, resist, and redefine law in formal and informal ways.

Many scholars have examined the role of automobility in vehicular society. Others have considered in great length the role that mobility and motion play in thinking of legal geography through kineticism and mobility.

Even as the car itself seems to take on human qualities of identity, of place occupancy, and of rights, the roadscape, as the medium for automobility, is the surface that enlivens our vehicular relationships to one another beyond what's officially sanctioned through driving manuals. Even as the car is basically (as my partner, a talented automobile mechanic notes) simply four wheels that either run or don't, the ability of the car to drive or not is based upon the prima facie of a paved infrastructure for smooth vehicular flow. It is this asphalted surface that sustains the legal materiality of pavement in the roadscape through the practices of using asphalt to govern each other in what I refer to as pavementality and pavementeering. As a legalized surface created for the four wheels of a car to travel upon as the focus of this book, I examine the roadscape as the site for which automobility is expected, the hybridized place in which kinetic mobility meets a stationary yet evolving surface, and the dynamics of the asphalted terrain are determined through motion yet remain themselves static. The law of the roadscape is enlivened through the pavement, pavementalities, and pavementeering. This paved medium of asphalt is a complex surface for legality that constitutively frames the order against disorder involving jurisdiction tensions, property ownership, and cultural identities in vehicular environments.

I have written extensively about the vehicular landscape as a fascinating medium for which to inhabit the life of law in everyday life. As my dissertation and then later a book, I considered the practice of parking as a source of law that helped define and contest socio-legal practices of rights, identity, and property.[1] Additionally, I have considered parking in terms of formal versus informal law through the socio-legal regulation of the American handicapped parking space[2] and the need of handicapped parking as an intentionally ignored site of post-9/11 regulations.[3] I have also considered the linear design of parking spaces[4] and drive thrus,[5] the legalized ambiguity of American yellow traffic lights,[6] the legal semiotic of the license plate,[7] driveways as a hybridized public/private space,[8] and the effectiveness of localized regulation when implemented by the driving public.[9] I have served on a parking appeals committee at a small New England college, as well as on the Chancellors Parking Committee at a larger state university, to address and reconsider the policy-based structures of parking permits, parking enforcement, and parking outlaws. As parking is the flipside to driving, parking involves the aesthetics of the stationary while driving is steeped in the aesthetics of motion. Yet whether in parking or in driving, pavement prevails as a common framework for both types of vehicular activity.

With much gratitude for providing the foundational enthusiasm for the original ideas developed in this book, I would like to also express my sincerest appreciation and warmest expressions of mahalo to Andreas Philippopoulos-Mihalopoulos, Christian Borch, and Colin Perrin for their continued support of my work and their faith in me despite those many curveballs that life throws. In helping to develop this project from its original inception as a chapter in my earlier book, *Law and the Kinetic Environment* (Routledge 2021), written for the *Space, Materiality, and the Normative* Series, I wish to thank the anonymous reviewers for their generous insights and constructive critiques. In providing some early research funding for this project, I wish to mahalo the College of Arts and Sciences at the University of Hawai'i Hilo for the CAS Faculty Small Research Grant I received during the summer of 2019. Mahalo, too, to Chris Lauer and the conference participants of the Pacific Association for the Continental Tradition (PACT), who heard early ideas for this project at UH Hilo in 2016; and Kirsten Møllegaard, Heather Neidhamer, Marilyn Brown, Lynn Morrison, Kathryn Besio, Peregrine Schwartz-Shea, Dvora Yanow, Farah Godrej, Anne Wagner, Marianne Takamiya, Jonathan Price, Su-Mi Lee, Anna Kennedy, and Biff Kennedy for their humor, strength, support, and generous insights. I wish to especially thank Kieran Tranter, an appreciated kindred spirit in vehicular research and writing about law and culture, for generously contributing his ideas and extensive knowledge to the Foreword of my book. Lastly, but certainly not the least, I would like to thank Jon, Harriet, and Olive for always, and willingly, getting in the car and going.

Notes

1 Marusek, Sarah. 2017. *Politics of Parking: Rights, Identity, and Property.* New York: Routledge. First published by Ashgate in 2012.
2 Marusek, Sarah. 2005. "Wheelchair as Semiotic: Space Governance of the American Handicapped Parking Space." *Law Text Culture* 9: 177–88.
3 Marusek, Sarah. 2007. "Between Disability and Terror: Handicapped Parking Space and Homeland Security at Fenway Park." *International Journal for the Semiotics of Law* 20 (3): 251–61.
4 Marusek, Sarah. 2020. "Parking Policy: The Socio-Legal Architecture of Parking Bays in American Cities." *Land Use Policy* 91: 103931.
5 Marusek, Sarah. 2019. "Coffee and the Queue: Linear Normativity and Vehicular Flow of the American Drive-Thru." *Lo Squadarno: Explorations in Space and Society* 52: 51–54.
6 Marusek, Sarah. 2014. "Visual Jurisprudence of the American Yellow Traffic Light." *International Journal for the Semiotics of Law* 27 (1): 183–91.
7 Marusek, Sarah. 2016. "License Plates: Personalized Jurisdiction and Performativity of Rights." *Law, Culture, and the Humanities* 12 (3): 566–81.
8 Marusek, Sarah. 2012. "Lawnscape: Semiotics of Space, Spectacle, and Ownership." *Social Semiotics* 22 (4): 447–58.
9 Marusek, Sarah 2016. "The Aloha Paradox: Law and Culture in Hawai'i." *Space and Polity* 21 (1): 108–22; Marusek, Sarah, and John Brigham, eds. 2017. *Street-Level Sovereignty: The Intersection of Space and Law.* New York: Lexington.

Foreword: On the Road

The great American novel is important. The United States is a nation that is intensely aware of its origin stories involving pilgrims, rights and revolution, manifest destiny, and global exceptionalism. It is aware that it is *made*, constructed by act and contract, by being written. It is a narrated polis. The novel is intertwined with nation (Buell 2014).

For me, the greatest American novel of the 20th century is Jack Kerouac's *On the Road* (Kerouac 1957). It captures the color and beat of a diverse and grand nation inhabited by less-than-perfect people (Swartz 1999). Foremost, the novel rolls, as the title suggests, on the road (Cresswell 1993). If 19th century America was made through railways and steam, 20th century America was made by the road and the car (Flink 1976).

Kerouac's novel has a profound engagement with what could be identified as living with automobility and the nascent counterculture (Collins and Skover 2013). It also invokes a liminal sense of law. Sal Paradise and Dean Moriarty are askew to the laws of the land and the norms of post-war white middle America. Perpetrators of minor maleficence relating to property, the road rules, liquor and drugs, they also embody a masculine rejection of domesticity and settling down (Delgado 2013). If jurisprudence in the 20th century could be seen as existing in a tension between three poles – the institutions of sovereign violence and posited orders, the bad man and the social of lived legality, and an awareness of the power, bodies, and subjectivities that infuse that lived legality – then *On the Road* could be read as textbook: a roadmap to the imaging and theorizing of the legal in the American gasoline century.

It is on the road as a material experience of movement and legality that Sarah Marusek brilliantly captures in this book. The roadscape – for Marusek, the assemblage emergent from asphalt, signs, and lines and the normative commitments needed for the vehicles to keep rolling – is seemingly innocuous and not seen. Normally roads and the legalities that support them, the legalities imposed by them, and the forms of techno-mobile consumption anticipated and encouraged by them, are just there. Only seen and front-of-mind when absent. The pothole that jars and disrupts smooth travel. Or the road to be built over in disregard of a local community's concerns. The roadscape is the habitus for modern life. While there is seemingly endless focus on transformations of the digital in contemporary popular and legal discourses, the roadscape, as an established techno-legal construct, has faded from view. All the contemporary concerns with how the digital, as meta, as AI, as surveillance techno-totalities, *might* change human lives seem immaterial when the roadscape structures how lives are lived in the immediate and present.

Marusek makes roads visible. The physicality of the road surface, its color and texture, its delineations of lanes and shoulders, of signs and sights is something that Marusek brings to the forefront. She maps how the engineered and planned forms of a road interact with laws and cultures. The road is marked both by laws but also through a shared culture of use. The road is generally a public good – a commons – on which and through the polis moves. The arteries of the nation. This fundamental awareness of the good of roads explains many of the complexities associated with private roads and obstructions on roads. In doing so, Marusek does what many who are not road construction engineers might not see as possible: she makes roads interesting and layered in meaning.

Studies in automobility and law – including my own – have underestimated the road. The emphasis has been on the noisy, shiny, attention-grabbing machine: the motor vehicle in all its complex signification. The car and its laws, its incorporation into modes of governing, forms of hypermobile life, and its gendered expressions have been the focus (Tranter and Martin 2013; Tranter 2014; Doyle and Tranter 2015). The road, where it is considered, is just b(l)ack(s)top. Just there. The stage on which dreams and fears of mechanized life and its norms are played out. By making the reader slow down and look at the road as a moment in the landscape that requires engagement, Marusek reveals the pavement as deeply political.

To lay a road is to make a claim of control. It is a sovereign act of power. The celebrated woodblock print in the front matter of Hobbes' *Leviathan* (Hobbes 2008) has a road connecting the town to the country and then snaking up a valley seemingly connecting to the torso of the sovereign standing over its world. The road seems to flow from sovereign, connecting the habitats on the land to the habitual lord of it all. Furthermore, as Marusek emphasizes in the chapter on 'pavementality,' the power is not just in the making of roads but in the authorizing of who can travel. The bypass makes it easier for people at A to get to B, but not those at C. Roads connect populations and communities but also preferences some over others. The history of highway construction in the United States and the wider West has been the story of accelerated urbanization. Country and land as inconvenience to an urbanized majority whose lives are dedicated to the compression of spacetime. The road, especially the straight modernism of the freeway with its overpasses and exit ramps, impose a mode of being in motion onto the landscape. There is another less essential and more mundane politic at play in Marusek's discussion of pavementality. The power and politics of the pothole. Not only has it seeped into the vernacular for the disruption of well-laid plans (we've hit a pothole), but potholes and their repair are high stakes for municipal authorities. Failure to maintain roads as pothole-free is seen as a repudiation of the social contract by the voter-motorists of America.

However, there is something highly specific emergent in the power at play in the contemporary American road. The Roman Empire was famously built on roads of gravel and stone. The American epoch, and with it, Western dreams of freedom and consumption are built on asphalt. Asphalt is poured onto country, hot and sticky to harden into semipermanence. It is a demarking and an owning, a marking of the land and an ordering of how to travel. As monuments to power and a particular governing order, roads are vulnerable to counter politics. As Marusek shows in relation to the rock protests on the access road to the proposed Thirty Meter Telescope on the sacred to Native Hawaiians Mauna O Wakea, to impede the flow of traffic is also a political act. The road as a symbol of a colonializing sovereignty and as infrastructure for social and economic exchange makes it a site of resistance. Climate change activities throughout the West are obstructing freeways. To block a road is to push back against Leviathan and its authorized forms of consumption. It interrupts that polis in anticipation of laying a new one.

Marusek's focus is explicitly on the road in the United States. However, her conceptualization of the semiotics of the road that open to forms of life made possible through and by roads, to sovereign violence and its contestation around road making and road obstruction, have utility beyond the land of the brave and mechanized free. The planet has been on the road, rolling along with Sal Paradise and Dean Moriarty, for a century. While there have been nuanced differences in the way that the road had spread and formed human lives – as sometimes acknowledged by the automobility literature (Clarsen and Veracini 2012) – Marusek's schema is particularly useful. It connects the immediate material forms and habitual cultural practices of road use to the social and the sovereign.

I was, appropriately, reading Marusek's text on a road trip. An Australian who lives on Yugambeh First Nation country (Gold Coast in South East Queensland), we were journeying during Easter 2022 to Gunggari country along the Maranoa River (the town of Mitchell in Western Queensland), a round trip of more than 900 miles. The land changed from subtropical rainforest to bread-bowl cropping, to over the Great Dividing Range and onto cattle and coal country, with bright red dirt and deep blue skies (Figure 0.1). A settler state where the colonizing project is evident, contested, and resisted (Blagg and Anthony 2019), the roads reach out like skeletal fingers from the coast into the bush. Where the United States is narrated, Australia is imposed from elsewhere, a bureaucratic decision of the English military-industrial elites to displace populations and impress a radically different governing order onto an ancient land. Its roads are where the violence and death of the imposition are manifested. Every few miles, a smashed and mutilated kangaroo ringed by a murder of big black crows (Simpson 2006). There were many crushed and mangled vehicles discarded just off the road shoulder. And throughout massive B-triple semi-trailers, over 115 feet in length, kinetic leviathans patrolling the blacktop, pumping black diesel smoke into the sky as they power up through the gears. This is the road and car culture that gifted the world the Mad Max franchise (Falconer 1997; Tranter 2020; Kitson 2003). Brutal agents of an itinerant sovereignty rushing violently across country (Clarsen 2017).

Figure 0.1 On the Road in Western Queensland (April 2022, after rain). Photograph by the author

To see the violence of occupation by a contested sovereign and its massive mechanicalized sentries is also to miss the beauty of the land and the communities connected by what really are only thin lines on the map. There are counter roads that have a different speed and different forms of life. Immediately, the asphalt – bitumen in the Australian vernacular (confusing for road engineers) – runs out on the side roads, as dirt in various stages of grading and eroding become the dominant medium. These roads demand less speed and more awareness of the country. There is more a being in rather than powering through (Frederick and Stefanoff 2011). Then there is the ever-present sense of the songlines of care for country by the First Nation peoples (Higgins 2021). Below the veneer of fences and introduced species, the marks on a shield tree, a fossick at the edges of a dirt road that always reveals a shaped stone tool, and a resurgent counter sovereignty in the assertion of names and language, present a visibility that this country can be traveled and cared for in ways radically different to the settler state.

This is the gift that Marusek has provided in this book. A way to see and think the road that is nuanced, provocative, and rich. A way to understand the road and the human lives that it makes and takes away as it is, in its concrete materialism. But also, a schema through which to glimpse its transformations and potentialities.

Kieran Tranter, Professor, School of Law,
Queensland University of Technology

Reference List

Blagg, Harry, and Thalia Anthony. 2019. *Decolonizing Criminology.* Basingstoke: Palgrave Macmillan.

Buell, Lawrence. 2014. *The Dream of the Great American Novel.* Harvard: Harvard University Press.

Clarsen, Georgine. 2017. " 'Australia – Drive It Like You Stole It': Automobility as a Medium of Communication in Settler Colonial Australia." *Mobilities* 12 (4): 520–33.

Clarsen, Georgine, and Lorenzo Veracini. 2012. "Settler Colonial Automobilities: A Distinct Constellation of Automobile Cultures?" *History Compass* 10 (12): 889–900.

Collins, Ronald K. L., and David M. Skover. 2013. *Mania: The Story of the Outraged and Outrageous Lives That Launched a Cultural Revolution.* Oak Park, IL: Top Five Books.

Cresswell, Tim. 1993. "Mobility as Resistance: A Geographical Reading of Kerouac's 'On the Road'." *Transactions of the Institute of British Geographers* 18 (2): 249–62.

Delgado, Richard. 2013. "Two Narratives of Youth." *Seattle University Law Review* 37.

Doyle, Kylie, and Kieran Tranter. 2015. "Automobility and 'My Family' Stickers." *Continuum: Journal of Media and Cultural Studies* 29 (1): 70–83.

Falconer, Delia. 1997. "We Don't Need To Know the Way Home: The Disappearance of the Road in the Mad Max Trilogy." In *The Road Movie Book*, edited by Steven Cohan and Ina Rae Hark, 249–70. London: Routledge.

Flink, James J. 1976. *The Car Culture*. Cambridge, MA: MIT Press.

Frederick, Ursula, and Lisa Stefanoff. 2011. "Emerging Perspectives on Automobilities in Non-Urban Australia: A Context for Cruising Country." *Humanities Research* 17 (2): 1–16.

Higgins, Noelle. 2021. "Songlines and Land Claims; Space and Place." *International Journal for the Semiotics of Law* 34 (3): 723–41.

Hobbes, Thomas. 2008. *Leviathan*. New York: Pearson Longman. 1651.

Kerouac, Jack. 1957. *On the Road*. London: Penguin.

Kitson, Michael. 2003. "The Great Aussie Car Smash at the End of the World." *Australian Screen Education* 31: 64–69.

Simpson, Catherine. 2006. "Antipodean Automobility and Crash: Treachery, Trespass and Transformation of the Open Road." *Australian Humanities Review* 39–40.

Swartz, Omar. 1999. *The View from On the Road: The Rhetorical Vision of Jack Kerouac*. Carbondale and Edwardsville: Southern Illinois University Press.

Tranter, Kieran. 2014. "The Car as Avatar in Social Security Decisions." *International Journal for the Semiotics of Law* 27 (4): 713–34.

———. 2020. "The End of Fury Road." In *Law, Lawyers and Justice: Through Australian Lenses*, edited by Kim Weinert, Karen Crawley and Kieran Tranter, 258–74. Abingdon: Routledge.

Tranter, Kieran, and Damien Martin. 2013. "'The Cutting Edge of Cocking About': *Top Gear*, Automobility and Law." *Law and Humanities* 7 (1): 1–18.

1 Pavement

According to the National Asphalt Pavement Association, there are "over 2.6 million miles of paved roads in the United States, [and] over 94% of them are surfaced with asphalt" (National Asphalt Pavement Association n.d.). As a practical material for paving, asphalt is "versatile, cost-effective, high-quality, long-lasting, and provides a comfortable ride" (Virginia Asphalt Association n.d. a). Asphalt is the public choice for vehicular infrastructure as it can installed, repaired, and replaced with relative ease compared to the laying of concrete or cobblestone surfaces. Through its construction, usage, deterioration, and repair, asphalt as a surface of normative, ordered, linear flow is often interrupted by disorder and chaos. Through the contested governance of flow and the interruptions to that flow, the roadscape is an asphalted legal institution in which the corpus of law and legality can be metaphorically transcribed onto the asphalted body of a highway's arteries or the shoulders of a paved road. As legal metaphor, the asphalted roadscape with its surface intended for vehicular occupancy, for vehicular speed, and vehicular travel is a hegemonic Americanized institutional surface for compliance, governance, and rebellion. The asphalted surface of the roadscape provides a canvas for the public habitus of cars, drivers, formal and informal law on the surface of the vehicularized environment (Bourdieu 1986; Di Palma 2016).

While many have conceptualized of the relationship of car to person to society (Cresswell and Merriman 2011; Featherstone, Thrift, and Urry 2005; Seo 2019; Sheller 2018; Vinsel 2019), the road itself, as the literal foundation for cars to drive upon, compels further consideration as a site of socio-legal research (Merriman 2011; Merriman 2014; Hvattam et al. 2016). Similarly, asphalt, as a predominant medium for roadway surfaces, has been extensively studied for its physical qualities of strength and durability. Although the surface for vehicular travel could be gravel, concrete, brick, dirt, or even cooled lava rock, asphalt is the ubiquitous surface choice for parking lots, streets, and freeways. Paved ribbons of asphalt delineate

DOI: 10.4324/9781315231853-1

Figure 1.1 "California's Big Sur Highway"

the contemporary landscape of the United States, one of many countries throughout the world in which cars and the people inside them represent a humanity in motion on asphalted terrain. Therefore, the roads on which cars drive perpetuate a unique legal landscape in which the surface for motion invites tensions from its occupants. The car is the preferential inhabitant of the paved vehicular space. However, not just any car is encouraged to inhabit the roadscape; instead, the vehicle in motion is the invited guest. Not all cars are in motion, with many parked at rest waiting to be driven once again (Ben-Joseph 2012). Parked cars represent a different understanding of mobility insofar as a parked car is not a car that engages in stop and go motion, such as in a traffic jam. Parked cars reveal an aesthetic of the stationary, in which the asphalt beneath the car belongs only to that parked car. The parked car is not in motion; however, it is through the aesthetics of motion of cars in general that the roadscape exists. Hence the subsequent relationship of driving to a surface of asphalt beckons further examination into this idea, this practice and to this place. In considering this dimensionality, the roadscape is a framework in which the conceptualization of motions happens from the ground up. Literally, if we consider the role that pavement, usually asphalt, plays in the vehicular landscape of the contemporary United States and in other places that might be similar, the roadscape is the site of legal geography in which motion, automobility, and govern-mentality (Foucault 1991) develop one another. Just as driving has its rules and customs, so too does the asphalted foundation for cars: the pavement.

Everyday vehicular environments involving roads jurisprudentially con-structs kinetic understandings of how law is perceived, place is constructed, and both are responded to. In his book *Traffic: Why We Drive the Way We Do*, Tom Vanderbilt (2008) considers the road as the foundation for vehicu-lar socialization, which he refers to as traffic, or the flow of cars on a road. In the fields of legal geography and automobility, the car is often consid-ered a source of informal law that serves as an anthropogenic representation of formal order within Western society. Kylie Doyle and Kieran Tranter (2017) remind us that law can be seen on the motor vehicle itself as visual jurisprudence is found in bumper stickers and other vehicular assemblages. Peter Merriman (2014, 202) asserts the roads are "a persistent – if rather banal – presence in many people's everyday lives, providing more-or-less clear demarcation of routes through variable topographies and/or land-scapes carved up by property owners." While roads do exist for purposes of transportation and access, roads themselves are an important site of legal geography for the sheer reason that the open, flat, smooth, linear pavement generates an understanding of law that is spatially informed.

The roadscape, or the paved asphalted surface that enlivens cultures of ownership, practices of territoriality, and jurisdictional assertions of power, is the paved vehicular environment of the road. As a surface for cars to drive upon from place to place, this asphalted terrain is designed with for-mal and informal law in mind, whether through painted surfaces, signage, or the noise of a honking horn. Even as the rules of the road range from state-issued driving instruction manuals to the lived experience of interact-ing with the pavement and with other drivers, the roadscape spurns a wild terrain of rule-breaking and contested understandings of what the lines, the signs, and the horn may mean. Particularly in the United States, everyday life is vehicularized, as we live in, around, between, and through cars. This vehicularization of daily life tethers de Certeau's (1984) consumerist prac-tices that sculpt our ordinary existence to Delaney's (2010) nomosphere in which the car, as well as the road as a site of travel, become techniques of world-making. Social order is governed through vehicular practice of spontaneous, fleeting interactions between drivers and the materiality of asphalted terrain that characterizes the roadscape. Interestingly, through motion, the car with a driver is not the same as a car without a driver, just as the road with a car is not the same as the road without cars. The anonymity between drivers of cars in transitional and transactional moments beckons a distinct understanding and application of law that contextually happens on the street. While formally there are traffic laws, informally, these laws may not be recognized and/or acknowledged given the localized determinations of conditions. Roads, be they heavily traversed or more remotely located, serve to determine the actions of drivers. The act of traveling is then associated with the freedom to move through the informal legalscape of the roadscape that governs the relationship of the car to the pavement (Merriman 2011).

Textures of the Asphalted Terrain

The roadscape is an environment for vehicular travel. As such, the asphalted pavement is specialized in its installation and its upkeep. As the surface immediately responsive to the revolving rubberized tire, the optimal texture of the roadscape is even, flattened, and straightened with a consistent width. Additionally, the surface is smooth enough to minimize unnecessary impacts to a traveling vehicle. Taking inclement weather into account, the texture of asphalt can be salted to melt accumulating snow or ice, grooved to lessen the possibility of hydroplaning during rainstorms, and consistently planned to lessen ponding, dips, or bumps. The climate's influence on the texture of the asphalt is closely tied to the need for high-speed travel on the

Figure 1.2 "Railroad Crossing"

preponderance of roads built for speed. On these types of roadscapes, the speed limit is posted to indicate the rate of safe travel based on textured nuances of the road's surface in the terrain of the roadscape. For example, on urban straightaways, the speed limit may be higher than on curvy mountain roads. In this way, the texturization of the pavement is based in the constructed line of the asphalt while taking into account the enveloping terrain in which the roadscape exists. The purpose of the pavement's texture is to facilitate smooth, even, and accelerated vehicular travel. Avoidable interruptions to the flow of travel can be achieved through the texture of asphalt that is conducive to travel associated with unencumbered forward acceleration. With a texture that takes the presence of water as well as physical upheaval of the pavement from below the surface of the asphalt into account, the navigation of the roadscape is eased through the straight and narrow (Ingold 2016). The banality of the roadscape's asphalted surface texture is key to uninterrupted vehicular flow.

Asphalt is a painted surface. Usually black or gray in color, asphalt is primed for white or yellow paint. The contrast from dark to light provides a reference point for navigation of the surface and the regulation of asphalted spaces. Whether as lane lines, a designated shoulder, or arrows directing travel, paint on asphalt is an aesthetic of governance in which driveability is designated according to the presence of the painted line, the solidity of the painted line, and the legal semiotic of the image painted on the asphalt's surface. Painted lines and images convey specific meanings for the regulated usage of the asphalt. The colors and designs of paint on asphalt are intentionally standardized (Wagner 2006; Ewing and Brown 2009). For example, a solid double yellow line in the middle of the pavement would direct a two-way flow of traffic without the allowance for faster cars passing slower cars; however, a broken yellow line, or a linear sequence of yellow dashes, in the center of the road would allow the safe passing of slower vehicles. Another example would be the solid white painted line on the exterior sides of the road in which to designate the intentional space of the road's shoulder. Travel to the left of that white line would be based upon speed whereas in contrast, travel to the right of the solid white line would indicate the need to interrupt travel or to stop the vehicle in the safe normativity of the shoulder. However, even as lines can be broken or paint can fade, painted asphalt is a limitation of vehicular regulation; drivers often do cross the solid yellow line while passing as well as drive on the shoulder of the roadscape during traffic jams or if the vehicle is damaged for whatever reason. The neutrality of the white or yellow painted asphalt is a façade of governance insofar as the logic expected to be employed by drivers in navigating the roadscape is a form of common sense that we all abide by, but not completely. Wide painted white lines that designate a pedestrian crosswalk pose an interruption to the flow of vehicular travel that many drivers ignore. The imperative of interrupting acceleration to slow down, if not simply stop, for a pedestrian in a crosswalk does not always happen. One alternative to the ignored rule of the wide white painted lines of the crosswalk is the illegal yet ubiquitous practice of jaywalking. Jaywalking, or crossing the road outside the legal designation of pedestrian space, is the acknowledgment that painted governance has its limits.

The shoulder lane, or the lane that is the designated space to pause travel located on the right side of the roadway and designated by a solid white line, provides a spatial break from the normative speeding motion of travel that takes place within the lanes. The shoulder is the spatial acknowledgment that speed is not absolute, and that de-acceleration must accompany acceleration. Spatial occupancy of the shoulder is temporary in expectation as the shoulder is not a parking space, except in an emergency situation in which a car and its motion break down. The shoulder lane provides a respite in the roadscape as a place to pause the motion of travel. Law enforcement relies upon the shoulder as a space in which to pull over vehicles. Some states have laws that require motorists traveling in the lanes to change lanes to allow the shoulder occupants even further space away from speeding vehicles. Tow trucks that come to the aid of disabled vehicles rely upon the shoulder to assist the driver and remove the vehicle from the constant motion of the roadscape. The shoulder provides a spatial intermediary for respite from motion, as the boundary between motion and stoppage is the solid white line that can be crossed if needed. In considering the embodied aspects of the roadscape, the shoulder is the support system for constant motion, for as the lane in which motion can temporarily stop, motion continues but is not an absolute imperative for the vehicular occupancy of the roadscape. Through the buttressing of the road's shoulder akin to the shoulders of the human body, the mobility of the roadscape is upheld through the support system afforded to drivers through the possibility of stopping in the shoulder lane. Yet not all roadscapes have shoulders; some roads only have a middle yellow stripe demarcating two-way opposing traffic. Conceptually, however, the practice of the shoulder can be in the grassy side areas of the roadscape in which a car in motion could pull over to "rest". The grassy lane, or gravel lane, is the expansion of the paved jurisdictional practice of the shoulder extending into the non-paved terrain that creates the expanse of the roadscape. There is usually width to allow for the deviation from constant motion om most roadscapes with a shoulder, or support zone, that frees the motion from acceleration to stoppage. In this way, the roadscape allows for non-travel for vehicles in motion. Nonetheless, the shoulder is not the same as a parking lot, where the purpose of the space is a car without a driver. Unlike when leaving a parked car, drivers who stop on the shoulder are legally expected to remain with their vehicle until help arrives with the purpose of moving that stopped vehicle from the general flow of traffic.

However, just as the roadscape involves the refuge of a shoulder lane, the curb of a roadscape involves the physical demarcation of vehicular space from non-vehicular space. Generally found on roadways with slower, intermittent travel, such as streets in urban or residential areas, the curb signals the boundary of vehicular space from pedestrian space. Usually a concrete or asphalt mound, the physicality of the raised curb is intended to stop the motion of cars and effectively corral cars in the motile areas of the roadscape. Delineating car space from people space, the curb can cause hoped-for damage to a moving car that hits the curb. As a deterrent to driving on the sidewalk or otherwise trespassing into pedestrian space, the curb literally "curbs" the free-range capacity of a car in motion within a curbed linear area for vehicular flow. Yet, the intentional ignoring of the curb boundary, referred to as "jumping the curb," can result in pedestrian injury and death. The curb fosters a borderland (Jones 2012) within the roadscape between moving car and walking person in areas of flow. In areas with reduced flow, the curb contributes to the public good, insofar as curbside parking is the optimal parking space as resource in consumer areas, because the turnover of cars is higher when drivers don't have far to walk between their car and their destination (Shoup 2011). However, in areas of flow within the roadscape, the curb has the same purpose, namely, to deter vehicular movement. As the equivalent of a curb in a roadscape in which people are present on the road, such as at a construction site, enormous concrete barriers which resemble giant curbs serve as a heightened barrier between the stationary and the motile. The intention is the same, namely, to safeguard pedestrian space from the speed of vehicular motion.

While vehicular motion seems to be a constant in the roadscape, the vehicular environment is more than just the constant of a linear physicality of flow in reaching a destination. Sometimes the destination is simply the flow itself, insofar as the flow of the roadscape provides a level of escapism within this atmospheric space of acceleration. One can enter the roadscape with the intention of escaping through the motion of travel. The escapism of the road is a common Hollywood theme in which the fluidity offered by the road is the solution to insolvable problems: just get in the car and drive. The roadscape is the site of freedom and liberty, not only in Hollywood films (including *Fast and the Furious* and *Thelma and Louise* as but two examples among many others), but in everyday life through the cultural phenomenon of the American road trip. The road trip is based upon getting a car and driving and stopping when the urge strikes (Schlereth 1985). However, the ability to exit the roadscape to grab a meal, visit a monument, or spend the night in a hotel is framed around the exit ramp. Getting off the expressway is dependent upon the construction of a ramp in which the traveling vehicle can slow down before coming to a stop at the end of the exit ramp. The intentional slowing down of travel that the exit ramp provides is an alternative to the speed encouraged by the roadscape. The gradual decrease of speed is complemented by the gradual increase of speed that starts the vehicular motion in the roadscape. Resuming the flow can either be at the entrance to the roadscape or at a roundabout. The roundabout is a hybridized space in which entry as well as exit from the roadscape can either occur or not occur if a driver keeps driving around in the circularity of the roundabout. Knowing when to merge and when to let other drivers merge is the larger semiotic of the roundabout that serves as a form of legal communication between drivers in the otherwise comical circularity of the roundabout.

Yet, in contrast to the roundabout or the exit ramp, the roadscape abruptly stops at the intersection. Either involving a stop sign or a traffic light, the intersection stops the flow of travel to allow the crossing of the roadway. Travel is intersected by the perpendicularity of a flow. To regulate the conflicting point of these intersecting flows, the traffic light or stop sign is erected. Yet even this stoppage reflects the routinization of travel in the roadscape. The negotiation of this routine activity of stopping and going involves the law insofar as the fleeting spontaneity of deciding how to react at the points of stoppage has become a form of legal knowledge acquired most efficiently through vehicular experience. Formal law is limited in its dictation of the roadspace as the interactions between occupants of the roadscape are not always prescribed or enacted based on what is written in the driver's manual. Instead, the negotiation of the roadscape is a negotiation of the contextualized occupation of vehicular space. The culture of automobility is the larger outcome of these negotiations, particularly as the culture of pavement is a larger statement about how law works in American life as demonstrated on the nooks and crannies of the roadscape.

Surface Tensions

The terrain of the roadscape is constructed with the layering of purpose. From the outset, the roadscape invites a closer look into the pavement as the extension of government. As a demonstration of public infrastructure, asphalt literally paves the way for expectations of a vehicular normative mobility. Providing a stable foundation for cars to drive upon allows government, via public tax monies, to determine where roads should be and where the paved territoriality of law exists. While the visibility of law in the roadscape is in signs and painted lines on the pavement, the law is also fundamentally present through the initial existence of the road in particular

Figure 1.3 "Don't Litter!"

places. Law is intentional in its construction of the roadscape and through this intention, law's purpose is layered with public responsiveness to the needs of a vehicular society, with claims to land made through paving over what was initially dirt, grass, and lavarock. The designated usage of land, according to the paved terrain, reveals the purpose of the roadscape to be the intentional directing of vehicular travel in carving out the ground of power and control through asphalt in previously unpaved areas. In this way, the paving of asphalted roads is a statement of might, as the power to pave is also the power to govern. Accordingly, then, the roadscape's purpose is the building and maintenance of public infrastructure for cars as a demonstration of a government that is responsive to its vehicular constituents. What this does is to instill and perpetuate the presence of cars and the ability of cars to travel through the ever-expanding maze of paved roads as a normative landscape of vehicular hegemony. Finally, the purpose of building roads and generating the roadscape is to make this visibility of governance a basis for the linear aesthetic (Ingold 2015) that standardizes forward motion on smooth asphalted surfaces. Government is present if the road is smooth as well as if it is rough insofar as law is represented, either through function and responsiveness or through deterioration. Furthermore, whatever landscape existed prior to paving is changed once pavement takes hold. Land and usage of that land are subjected to the paved whims of the roadscape that dictate which roads will go where. In this way, the paved road reveals that the asphalted road is the territory of law, with law represented through taxation, government coffers, and governmental determinations of where roads should be built. The road itself, as the paved terrain of law, is a dynamic site between law, place, and power.

The surface tensions of pavement in the roadscape engender a site of cultural architecture that constructs cultural identities and everyday jurisprudence through the concept of travel and usage. The relationship between travel, pavement, and culture is premised upon motion but is peppered with the obvious counter to motion, which is the need to stop. Interrupting motion is a cultural statement tied to understandings of race, of place, and zones of travel, be they urban, rural, or a combination of the two. From jaywalking to hitchhiking to the crosswalk, the car serves as a protective bubble of motion, shielding the driver in an encased, motile setting. Of particular interest is how the drive-thru as a vehicularized queue and space has developed from ordering fast food into virus testing for Covid-19 during the 2020 pandemic. Travel is a socio-legal concept that is premised upon the roadscape, as the roadscape is constructed to define, facilitate, guide, colonize, and even restrict travel. The road signs of organizations that seek to adopt a stretch of road are political places in which the vehicularized application of speech and history is the catalyst for law and resistance to pavement as a method of interpreting the roadscape.

Just as the horizontality of the asphalt through paint or the texture of the surface is a source of legal governance, the signage that verticalizes the roadscape is an upright medium for communication. Usually at a distance of six to ten feet, road signs are a legalized method of visibly yet passively regulating the vehicular response and activity that normatively transpires within the roadscape. Road signs convey speed limit, upcoming curves and bends in the road, the potential for wildlife, bicycles, or children to be in the road, directions and stops along the way, the nature of a road's jurisdiction through its numerical identity (ex. Interstate I-95), or the upcoming presence of road construction. Colors are a vital aspect of road signs, with yellow urging caution, red calling for a complete vehicular stop, green often providing directions, blue providing public services, orange designated for road construction, or white as a routine expectation of asphalted regulations in the roadscape. The purpose of the sign is to forecast what might occur in the roadscape, whether as road conditions or vehicular knowledge of what's coming ahead. Signs symbolize the culture of pavement insofar as the pavement is a metaphor for the socio-legal reckoning of social interactions through the transportive bubble of the car (Jappy 2013). The sign provides a legal forecast for the momentum of the roadscape, for as the car travels on the road, road signs educate the driver about pavement-based conditions and likely occurrences. The serendipity of the roadscape suggests that the road itself provides the foundation for commonsensical approaches to risk that are legally anticipated as probable. What this means is that to account for the upcoming curves of a road, signage will indicate upcoming curves. The sign describes the road in ways that the driver should respond to accordingly. The communication of such dangers and risks is law's method to legalize the navigation of the roadscape through visible, erect semiotics of vehicular communication. Such signs also use the road-scape as a literal avenue for communication involving the roadscape. This latter type of sign enforces automobility as the intended inhabitation of the roadscape by providing further tools to extend the automobility of the road-scape as a conceptual communicative tool for social interaction and legal engagement with authority and regulation.

The standard of the vehicular terrain is a standard of smoothness. This architecture of the smooth, found in roads that are initially paved with asphalt, glosses over the textured surface of the vehicular terrain. The presumption that a road would be paved with asphalt dates to 625 B.C. Babylon (Cervarich 2001). "Asphalt has been around since the dinosaurs," as Margaret Cervarich, spokeswoman for the National Asphalt Pavement Association at the beginning of the twenty-first century, noted (D'Errico 2001). According to the Virginia Asphalt Association (n.d. b), the ancient Greeks used asphalt, or a mixture of asphalt, sand, and limestone, for sur-facing roads, with the word *asphaltos* meaning "secure" in ancient Greek. Asphalt pavement, a common surface for vehicular terrain, provides solidity to the contemporary road surface. Importantly, this surface can be repaved as needed, with a nod to a once-again smooth surface. The smoothness of pavement is a standard for smooth, ordered vehicular flow in the roadscape. The ordered, smooth paved terrain allows the uninterrupted flow of cars on the surface, ensuring that the driver focuses on the aesthetics of travel rather than navigating bumps, pits, and potholes. The aesthetics of travel include driving with other drivers while in traffic, navigating directions for travel, and also negotiating the aesthetics of the paved. If the aesthetics of travel are dependent upon motion and relationship to place and other cars, then the aesthetics of the paved pertain to ways in which the smooth road is in fact ordered for smooth travel. Signage, colors, lines, and width of the paved terrain help a driver to fully relate to what the road itself is trying to communicate. A smooth road communicates seamless expectations for driving. The laws of driving take a smooth road surface for granted, insofar as the prioritization of driver education is in reading the signs, interpreting the colors and the lines, and the positionality of the car itself on the road. The surface of the road is presumed to be smooth and therefore, neutral, and not of concern.

What makes a surface smooth or rough? The vehicular experience of driving gives a terrain texture. Texture is in this way the texture of feeling or experience while riding in a car. When a revolving tire is in contact with a road's surface, the riders in a car give the road texture. However, that feeling may be a function of the car itself (with working shocks and struts) rather than the surface of the road. Nonetheless, from a visual perspective, the texture of the vehicular terrain generally either looks smooth or looks bumpy. Rough roads, or roads that have a lot of potholes, uneven/broken asphalt, or are comprised of gravel as a surface medium, are roads that represent disruption to the flow of the smooth. The visual elements of smooth or rough give another dimension of texture to the road as a road that is more or less traveled. Furthermore, the dependency of the paved road as a foundation for vehicular travel reveals that the architecture of the smooth, as well as the rough, is a metaphor for law. Order through smooth operation is a legal metaphor for a society in which law maintains order through order (Simon 2007). Well-lit roads are also a function of smooth travel, as the visibility of the road surface becomes apparent in dim or absent lighting. Seeing the smoothness or roughness of the road is a dimension of the texture of the vehicular terrain, just as lighting on public streets is linked to a decrease in crime (Jacobs 1992). The responsiveness of government to the paved road as an attended public resource is inextricably linked to the visible surface quality of the asphalt. The pavement's deterioration, or roughened surface, is similar in perception to the (un)responsiveness of law to readily address, or conversely ignore, societal woes and/or problems with legal remedy.

In contrast, a bumpy or pitted road surface becomes the focus of a driver in such a rough terrain. Whether to protect the vehicle from bumpy disruptions that are driven over without realization, or as a way to pay strict attention to what the car is literally driving over, a bumpy road is chaotic. While a bumpy road can be smooth, the bumpiness of a rough road is not uniform. The chaotic, unexpected, random ramming of bumps, rough pavement, or potholes on a road's surface can be jarring to the smooth expectation of travel. This jarring can also take away the focus of the driver from the aesthetics of the paved. In other words, signage, colors/lines, and dimensionality of the pavement take a backseat to a driver's focus on not hitting bumps or driving around protrusions or dips on the road's surface. Bumpiness or surface roughness can be interpreted as disruption and disregard for order, if not uniform evenness of travel on the road. The pitch of a road, the layering of pavement, and the uneven surface that ignores standards of consistent flat are symptoms of disrepair. A rough road is a legal semiotic of a society in financial disrepair as the municipal imagery of smooth, repaired, paved roads is missing. The roughness of the vehicular terrain is associated with the upheaval of socio-legal foundations in which smoothness glosses over troubling elements that can be paved over, such as vehicular poverty, the financial stability of local or state government to fund and maintain roads, and even the inability to deliver the public service that is represented by the smoothly paved road.

Yet as long as the ability exists for the vehicle to proceed, the surface could be considered to be a road. Whether or not that road is passable speaks to the roughness of the road. Furthermore, whether or not a car is able to travel over the road without popping a tire, able to not get stuck in ruts, travel over branches and rocks, or even accelerate to a reasonable degree when moving the car from place to place, the surface terrain can itself effectively prevent travel. Or the surface terrain, if rough enough, means successfully navigating travel would mandate a particular type of vehicle, such as a four-/all-wheel drive car with suitable tires and sufficient height of the tires to safely traverse. In this sense, not all asphalt roads are normatively smooth, as the deteriorating asphalted road may lose its ability to meet the smooth standard status quo.

In this way, the legal narrative of pavement is a shifting juxtaposition between order (smooth) and chaos (rough), with the transient middle (becoming rough or becoming smooth) as itself slippery and neither fully smooth nor fully rough. Within this binary is the slippery nature of the road, in which slippery may be too smooth and not rough enough in ensuring the level of friction needed to alleviate slip. Even excluding regular road maintenance, the surface of the roadscape reveals the larger role that roads play in the dynamism of a vehicular environment and socio-legal-cultural landscape. By considering the smooth, the rough, and the slippery, or the becoming of smooth and rough, the textured terrains of vehicular surfaces for travel reveal a vehicular-based cultural architectural foundation for order as well as chaos. Most paved roads start out smooth. Over time and through vehicular usage, roads deteriorate. Responsiveness to the binary of rough and smooth is an illusory misrepresentation of what lies in between the binary, in what I refer to as the *slippery*.

The binary of smooth versus rough asphalt is incomplete and insufficient to address the range of surfaces that fall on the spectrum of smooth and rough. Non-asphalted surfaces are common in vehicular terrains and range in variety as roadscapes of gravel, grass, deteriorating (but not broken-up) asphalt, concrete, recycled glass, tile, stone, rubberized composites, dirt, cobblestones, bricks, hardened lava rock on Hawai'i Island, and even frozen glaciers in Iceland. Yet even then, the smoothness of the terrain is paramount to the functioning travelability of a road. Although this range of surfaces might become slippery due to external weather conditions or too smooth of a surface, the aesthetics of travel take into account the aesthetics of the paved and the aesthetics of the rough as contributing elements to safe travel and driver navigability of the road itself as a terrain for travel. Safe travel is the ability to use the road while driving a car without needing to focus on the risks to the car and to the motion of the car that arise from a rough surface. Smooth roads are an expectation of a functioning and responsive government. However, governments that allow for off-road travel in undeveloped terrains on non-asphalted surfaces are also considered to be responsive, insofar as the off-road driving experience becomes a function of vehicular regulation rather than surface regulation through the architecture of the smooth. Driving off-road is presumed to be an activity based upon the driving of roughened, possibly impassable asphalt. Normatively, rough roads are not fully the negation of the smooth, but instead beckon the emergence of a new categorization of textured terrain within the roadscape. In the off-road terrain, the desired paved texture is one of bumps and jarring travel. Getting stuck in the mud or the snow or the ruts is associated with the terrain. Being off-road on a road or not on a road is the premise for travel and provides the texture of the off-road terrain that is traveled by an automobile. In an interesting statement on the vehicularization of Western culture, the off-road texture of the vehicular terrain reveals a preference, if not dependency, on the rough rather than the smooth. In fact, through the off-road textured terrain, a designated road as surface for travel is not necessary or even desired. The rough is welcomed as dangerous and risky, where the smooth is tamed, domesticated, boring. Americans associate off-roading with traversing the wilderness through the safety of their rugged vehicle. In this way, the understanding of the smooth juxtaposes compliance with rebellion (Campbell 2006). This legal narrative is based in narratives of whites settling the wild Western United States, in which indigenous people were envisioned to be either tameable or removable onto secure designated tracts of land. Hundreds of years later, the narrative of conquest remains the same, yet on the textured terrain of pavement as the frontier in question.

In the changing frontier of global climate change, the surface of the earth and the atmospheric movements are dynamic and unrestrained. One threat to the foundation of the smooth can occur during times of calamity in which the surface of the road is neither smooth nor rough, but slippery as it is literally covered by water or is rendered non-existent if destroyed by a landslide, mudslide, or active lavaflow. The textured terrains of the roadscape as banal site of ubiquitous accessibility for traveling vehicles is challenged through their accessibility and existence during times of calamity. Moreover, slippery challenges to the foundation of the smooth can be found in the unfilled pothole, as a blemish in the asphalt that creates a hole for motorists to drive around. Potholes are a source of cultural tension involving both rage and resignation in a variety of urban and rural settings. Potholes play a key role in understanding evolving relationships between municipal governments, public criticism, and political sway. If smooth, the road weighs on the side of order and efficient mobility, even to the extent of reaching a tyranny of standards as we expect roads to be smooth; however, if rough, the road is a site of architectural transiency and seems to lack the stability typically associated with the paved environment. As a foundation for law's engagement with a warming environment involving high tides, earthquakes, floods, wildfires, and even flowing lava, the smooth road is juxtaposed with the rough road in ways that metaphorically allow us to see law and how it operates when confronted with a dynamic and shifting environment. It is this dynamic environment that make the pavement slippery, from smooth to rough to impassable, remote, and even removable.

Even as the window serves as a window to the outside, the road itself predicates our understanding of how vehicular environments are constructed for intentional usages and points of access, communication, or jurisdiction through the asphalting of power and place. The roadscape, as I develop in this book, is a vehicular landscape focused upon the role that pavement plays as the constructed foundation of pavement for automobility. As a space that is usually paved with asphalt, the legal liminality of the vehicular environment can be examined in three primary ways. This first dimension of the roadscape in Chapter 1, "Pavement," considers the structural design of the vehicular environment as a paved public landscape insofar as the textures of this vehicular terrain provide an intentionally crafted surface for vehicular motion and interaction between cars and asphalt. The second dimension of the roadscape involves the surface tensions of the paved terrain involving paved territoriality, usage, and public memory in what I refer to as pavementality. Chapter 2, "Pavementalities," examines the use of pavement for jurisdictional assertions and legal communications through the medium of pavement. The third dimension of the roadscape involves the kineticism inherent to the paved vehicular environment as changes in surface construction determine the fluidity of asphalted understandings and practices of vehicular presence in a phenomenon I call *pavementeering*. In Chapter 3, "Pavementeering" is the laying of culture, ownership, and pavement that gives rise to the road as contested terrain through its construction, maintenance, and ultimate rejection. Because the asphalted vehicular environment is a roadscape of smooth surfaces, speed, and fleeting interactions between drivers that engenders this space as a site of socio-legal regulation and resistance, the roadscape is a rich site of legal geography with a host of complex legal semiotics that construct the terrain and our understanding of this linear paved ribbon of asphalt as the terrain of law.

Through the roadscape, the dynamic landscape of the vehicular environment is introduced. Pavement becomes a legal semiotic. Roads become sites of legal geography as the automobile environment characterizes the jurisprudential relationship between law and place. Roads are complex sites of transience in which humans engage with cars and law seeks regulation and control over fleeting interactions. The structural institution of the road with the implicit presence of the moving vehicle establishes a fluid understanding about the construction of this man-made, pavement-based society. In interesting ways, law is limited in such kinetic spaces despite myriad legal regulations of roadway activity. The legal design and construction of roads as paved terrains of legal geography is further challenged by the juxtaposition of motion with permanence. As a metaphor for law, roads, shifting terrains, and regulated mobility challenge the stability of the legal landscape and contribute to a larger constitutive relationship between legality, movement, and spatiality. In this way, the road is a dynamic vehicular landscape involving the jurisprudential layering of human usage, legal design/construction/maintenance, and earthen terrain.

Reference List

Ben-Joseph, Eran. 2012. *Rethinking a Lot: The Design and Culture of Parking.* Cambridge: MIT Press.

Bourdieu, Pierre. 1986. *Distinction: A Social Critique of the Judgement of Taste.* Translated by Richard Nice. New York: Routledge.

Campbell, David. 2006. "The Biopolitics of Security: Oil, Empire, and the Sports Utility Vehicle." In *Legal Borderlands: Law and the Construction of American Borders*, edited by Mary L. Dudziak and Leti Volpp, 351–80. Baltimore: John Hopkins University Press.

Cervarich, Margaret B. 2001. "Asphaltos, Asphaltus, Asphalt: The History of Today's Most Popular Pavement." *Hot Mix Asphalt Technology* 6 (6): 32–37.

Cresswell, Tim, and Peter Merriman. 2011. *Geographies of Mobilities: Practices, Spaces, Subjects*. Burlington, VT: Ashgate.

De Certeau, Michel. 1984. *The Practice of Everyday Life*. Translated by Steven Rendall. Berkeley: University of California Press.

Delaney, David. 2010. *Nomospheric Investigations: The Spatial, The Legal, and the Pragmatics of World-Making*. New York: Routledge.

D'Errico, Richard A. 2001. "Asphalt, 'the Versatile, Quiet Pavement,' Is Cheaper, Faster, and Better than Concrete." *Albany Business Review*, July 30, 2001. Accessed March 11, 2022. www.bizjournals.com/albany/stories/2001/07/30/focus1.html.

Di Palma, Vittoria. 2016. "Flows: Rivers, Roads, Routes and Cartographies of Leisure." In *Routes, Roads and Landscapes*, edited by Mari Hvattum, Janike Kampevold Larsen, Brita Brenna, and Beate Elvebakk, 27–43. New York: Routledge.

Doyle, Kylie, and Kieran Tranter. 2017. "F#ck Your Family! The Visual Juris-prudence of Automobility." *International Journal for the Semiotics of Law* 30: 1–22.

Ewing, Reid, and Steven J. Brown. 2009. *U.S. Traffic Calming Manual*. New York: Routledge.

Featherstone, Mike, Nigel Thrift, and John Urry. 2005. *Automobilities*. London: Sage.

Foucault, Michel. 1991. "Governmentality." In *The Foucault Effect: Studies in Governmentality*, edited by Graham Burchell, Colin Gordon, and Peter Miller, 87–104. Chicago: University of Chicago Press.

Hvattum, Mari, Janike Kampevold Larsen, Brita Brenna, and Beate Elvebakk. 2016. *Routes, Roads and Landscapes*. New York: Routledge.

Ingold, Tim. 2015. *The Life of Lines*. New York: Routledge.

———. 2016. *Lines*. New York: Routledge.

Jacobs, Jane. 1992. *The Death and Life and Great American Cities*. New York: Vintage.

Jappy, Tony. 2013. *Introduction to Peircean Visual Semiotics: A Visual Rhetoric*. New York: Bloomsbury.

Jones, Reece. 2012. *Border Walls: Security and the War on Terror in the United States, Israel, and India*. London: Verso.

Merriman, Peter. 2011. "Roads: Lawrence Halprin, Modern Dance and the Ameri-can Freeway Landscape." In *Geographies of Mobilities: Practices, Spaces, Sub-jects*, edited by Tim Cresswell and Peter Merriman, 99–117. Burlington, VT: Ashgate.

———. 2014. "Roads." In *The Routledge Handbook of Mobilities*, edited by Peter Adey, David Bissell, Kevin Hannam, Peter Merriman, and Mimi Sheller, 196–204. New York: Routledge.

National Pavement Asphalt Association. n.d. "Fast Facts." Accessed March 11, 2022. www.asphaltpavement.org/uploads/documents/GovAffairs/NAPA%20Fast%20Facts%2011-02-14%20Final.pdf

Schlereth, Thomas. J. 1985. *U.S. 40: A Roadscape of the American Experience*. Indianapolis: Indiana Historical Society.

Seo, Sarah. 2019. *Policing the Open Road: How Cars Transformed American Free-dom*. Cambridge: Harvard University Press.

Sheller, Mimi. 2018. *Mobility Justice: The Politics of Movement in an Age of Extremes*. London: Verso.

Shoup, Donald. 2011. *The High Cost of Free Parking, Updated Edition*. New York: Routledge.

Simon, Jonathan. 2007. *Governing through Crime: How the War on Crime Trans-formed American Democracy and Created a Culture of Fear*. New York: Oxford University Press.

Vanderbilt, Tom. 2008. *Traffic: Why We Drive the Way We Do (and What It Says about Us)*. New York: Alfred A. Knopf.

Vinsel, Lee. 2019. *Moving Violations: Automobiles, Experts, and Regulations in the United States*. Baltimore: Johns Hopkins University Press.

Virginia Asphalt Association. n.d. a. "Why Choose Asphalt?" Accessed March 11, 2022. https://vaasphalt.org/asphalt-facts/why-choose-asphalt-2/.

———. n.d. b. "The History of Asphalt." Accessed March 11, 2022. https://vaasphalt.org/the-history-of-asphalt/.

Wagner, Anne. 2006. "The Rules of the Road: A Universal Visual Semiotics." *International Journal for the Semiotics of Law* 19 (3): 311–24.

2   Pavementalities

In their examination of pedestrian crossings in urban Australia, Mohr and Hosen (2017, 78) note the "interactions between formal and informal law and regulation in defining appropriate 'region behavior.'" Mohr and Hosen's distinction between formal and informal law importantly calls to attention the role of experiential knowledge that moves beyond the knowledge of the roadscape that originates in formal driving manuals. The attention to the regional quality of behavior is important in framing the determining role that locality plays in understandings of jurisdiction. The practices of jurisdiction involving pavement as a practical and conceptual paved place result in the propertizing of the paved within the roadscape. Dorsett and McVeigh (2012, 98) describe legal place as "a practice of jurisdiction":

> Place is not, as might be thought, a matter of legally bounded physical space, but rather it is the work of legal ordering and relationship. Jurisdictional practices create legal places through engaging with the material world.

Through jurisdictional assertions, pavementality is the performative jurisdictional practice of propertizing pavement from constructed roadways for travel into the paved territory of identity through assertions of ownership. Theoretically, this process is made visible through visible application of street signs and vehicular-centric gestures involving the complex interplay between pavement, jurisdiction, and territorialization. Accordingly, this process of propertization involves these aspects of place, spatiality, and ownership as they transpire in fluid, localized settings. Although the normativity of the roadscape may appear to strive for hegemonic uniformity in creating and sustaining a neutral objective for legitimized vehicular travel, this paved public setting of the roadscape can also be localized through these practices of pavementality. Through the texturization of the paved terrain, dimensions of travel and purpose of roadscape insignia are considered vital

DOI: 10.4324/9781315231853-2

Figure 2.1 Seeing the Forest through the Pavement

for imparting a theoretical conceptualization of pavementality. With a nod to the Foucauldian concept of governmentality, pavementality is the public engagement with the asphalted surface of the roadscape. The pavement-driven social responses to pavement transmit knowledge of how law works according to the rules of the road within the built environment of the road-scape. This environment is a terrain built for kinetic, linear, normative responses to the fleeting negotiations of pavement-responsive enactments of vehicular legality.

Adopt-a-Highway

The first application of pavementality can be found in Adopt-a-Highway programs, as characterized through a 1990s *Seinfeld* television sitcom episode. More generally, Adopt-a-Highway programs are the voluntary and temporary claim of ownership over a designated stretch of asphalted pavement, usually a mile or two in length. In these segments of the roadscape, jurisdiction is privatized through the named distinction of a stretch of public highway in which the named party is responsible for the removal of trash from the roadway. Through this ongoing act of care in picking up any litter on the assigned mile of roadway, the pavement is named accordingly through a road sign labeled with name of the tending organization. The purpose of adopting a highway is to publicize the goodwill of the volunteering organization in keeping the roadside free of litter. As an extension of territoriality, the name appearing on the road sign is construed as a demonstration of jurisdiction through the public recognition of assuming the responsibility of cleaning up trash. However, as the *Seinfeld* episode keenly shows, this jurisdictional game is a limited facade of privatized, temporary ownership insofar as the public expectations of a road are problematized when changed by private interests.

In the 1997 *Seinfeld* episode "The Pothole," the eclectic character Cosmo Kramer drives his car on a New York City expressway and runs over a sewing machine that has been discarded on the road. Peeved by what he considers to be highway litter from the irresponsibility and mismanagement of local city government, Kramer decides to "adopt" a section of the expressway. In his adoption of Mile 114 on the fictitious "Arthur Burghardt Expressway," Kramer assumes a parental role in caring for the road as a parent would care for a child. He lovingly picks up trash and strives to improve drivers' experience on "his" stretch of highway as a type of possession. Kramer really wants to care for his designated mile and takes the road signs home to clean them. As cars speed past, he risks his life to retrieve a discarded soda can lying in the middle of the highway. As Kramer relishes what he perceives to be pleased smiles on passing drivers' faces as they speed past him while he is on the shoulder, he decides to widen the lines for Mile 114 from four lanes down to two. Driving slowly as he leans out the window, he repaints them from his car. Although his friend, Elaine, drives by and remarks on the luxury of such wide lanes, complete chaos from the lane change ensues. Kramer's attempts to improve the experience of drivers along this stretch of adopted highway through the removal of street signs for cleaning, the restriping of lane lines to make them wider, and the risking of his own life darting in and out of traffic to keep the pavement free of litter, prove to be too much in the end. As he tries to return Mile 114 back to how it was, Kramer attempts to remove his paint with paint thinner, but ends up spilling much of that flammable liquid on the pavement, igniting a fire from the sparks of a passing truck that has driven over a sewing machine that once again appears on the road.

Since the 1980s, Adopt-a-Highway programs have encouraged the litter removal on roads by local organizations that can advertise their group on road signs (Clark 1989). The Adopt-a-Highway road signs, similar in color and shape to Kramer's sign in Figure 1.1, serves the purpose of reciprocity as public advertisement for groups and litter removal by volunteers. Also referred to as Sponsor-a-Highway programs, groups can work with nearly every U.S. state's Department of Transportation to clean up trash and let those who are driving on that stretch of adopted highway know of a particular group's willingness to pick up litter. Keeping the roadway free of trash is a leading benefit from the program, while adding publicity to the recognition of participating groups. A wide variety of groups participate in Adopt-a-Highway programs, including charities, religious groups, political organizations, the incarcerated, corporations, and local businesses (www. adoptahighway.com). Initially a program to garner community volunteerism with the collection of roadside trash, such programs now serve as a useful marketing tool for economic interests in an age of corporate responsibility. It is this benefit of broadcasting an organization or business's role in taking care of the vehicular environment that serves as fundamental part of the success of Adopt-a-Highway programs across the United States, ironically even on roadways that remain littered despite the adoption. Through the state's sponsorship for private companies and groups to serve as roadside caretakers made public through those names appearing on the road signs, pavementality is operationalized through control over the roadscape. Effectively, these signs act as billboards on a smaller scale in terms of height and regulatory complexity. However, the identity of sponsoring groups is itself politically taken into account by a variety of states, due to visibility concerns of aligning with certain groups and organization. One group in particular that has challenged local restrictions of their denied involvement in adopt-a-highway programs around the county is the Ku Klux Klan.

As possibly the most infamous and historically violent white supremacist organization in the United States, the Ku Klux Klan (KKK) has sought on numerous occasions to adopt a highway. In the 1990s, courts in Arkansas[1] (1992), Texas[2] (1995), and Missouri[3] (1999) toyed with the complexity of the public road, state recognition, and private organizations as a public forum. As Montgomery (1999) describes, the larger issue in these cases is states denying the ability of the KKK to formally adopt stretches of highway out of concerns that the states would be seen as legitimizing the organization through the allowance of road signs with the organization's name on them. At issue in these cases was the understanding and implementation of the road as a public forum in a variety of approaches. In the first, the traditional public forum would involve such a stretch of highway to be "held in the trust for the use of the public" for purposes of communication and debate of public questions (Montgomery (1999, 564) citing *Hague v. CIO* 307 U.S. 496, 515 (1936)). The second type of public forum would be limited or designated forum in using the logic that some "public property which the state has opened for use by the public as a place for expressive activity" (Montgomery 1999, 566) citing *Perry Education Association v. Perry Local Educators Association* 460 U.S. 37, 46 (1983). The third type of public forum would be a non-public forum that "the State, no less than a private owner of property, has power to preserve the property under its control for the use to which it is lawfully dedicated" (Montgomery 1999, 568) citing *Davis v. Massachusetts* 167 U.S. 43 (1897). The larger question on this public roadway in each of the three aspects of considering the extent to which the public forum doctrine exists in Adopt-a-Highway programs is whether or not the road sign on the public roadway is public to the extent that travel and seeing out the car window represents a form of public communication represented through the name of the sponsoring organization as allowed by the state. Because this understanding of the road and the road sign in Adopt-a-Highway programs is based on the public visibility (and legitimization by the state) of particular viewpoints, not all names of organizations should be allowed to appear on Adopt-a-Highway signs, despite recent court rulings to the contrary. As the most recent KKK case in 2016 involving Georgia mentions,[4] the concern of the state in preventing the KKK from sponsorship in the Adopt-a-Highway program and based in the public perception of state-promoted affiliations evident in signage, was overruled by the Georgia Supreme Court on the grounds of protecting the longstanding white supremacist organization's First Amendment free speech rights. As Georgia Transportation Commissioner Keith Golden initially asserted, "The impact of erecting a sign naming an organization which has a long-rooted history of civil disturbance would cause a significant public concern" (Grinberg 2016). In his initial rejection letter to the KKK, Golden also noted, "Impacts include the safety of the traveling public, potential social unrest, driver distraction, or interference with the flow of traffic" (Eschner 2017). However, attracting the vision of the flow of traffic in viewing this sign is the whole point. Similar in scope to billboards that advertise goods and services (Gudis 2004) or billboards that make the public aware of missing persons (Morton 2016), the Adopt-a-Highway sign depends upon the flow of vehicles for constant visibility.

Just as the flow of sight manages the semiotics of signs on the road, the flow of the roadscape divided into lanes for travel is a spatial phenomenon akin to fluvial space, as suggested in Tim Ingold's work (Ingold 2016, Ingold 2015). Blomley (2011) also depicts the momentum of flow that happens on the linear terrain of the sidewalk in which the movement of pedestrians is the intention of this concrete spatial reserve. Loukaitou-Sideris and Ehrenfeucht (2009) describe the separation that is inherent to occupants of the sidewalk through the purpose of continuous walking as movement. It is this separation between the vehicular occupants of the roadscape that is emulated between cars in the lanes of a roadscape. Whether those lanes separate the flow of oppositional traffic on a two-lane road or separate passing traffic traveling in the same direction, the linear division of the roadscape into lanes is a spatially responsive regulation. The semiotics of the lane can be seen in the dotted white lane lines or the double yellow line. Each color and type of lines fosters each individual lane as a spatial subdivision of the roadscape. The conceptualization of space according to the lane lines transfers to social practices and cultural understandings of jurisdiction. For example, the phrase "stay in your lane" is a colloquial meaning that one should mind one's own business or not deviate from one's specific trajectory. Interestingly, the passing lane (or the absence of a passing lane) is a jurisdictional allowance (or disallowance) to "change lanes," or to deviate from the linear lane and move over into the passing lane. The straight and narrow of the lane need not be necessarily tied to the slow. The ability to change lanes speaks to different approaches to reaching a destination. As Kramer repainted the lane lines in the *Seinfeld* episode, the space changed from narrow and constricted to wider lanes with presumably more freedom. Kramer hoped that drivers would enjoy the experience of driving in wider lanes and appreciate his repainting his adopted mile of the roadscape. However, the expansion of the space within the lane lines served only to distress drivers who had less lane-age overall in which to travel. Ultimately, the lines on the pavement serve as regulatory boundaries for car space in mimicking the personal space of bodies as we culturally understand the lines to demarcate the acceptable occupancy of spatial parameters.

Rules of the Road

As linear space that intentionally and exclusively invites the routine occupancy of motorized vehicles, the roadscape is a built environment that is stable but flexible, and engineered with standards that result in dependable and familiar patterns. The roadscape affirms spatial normativities associated with the asphalt and driving the car on the surface of that asphalt in ways recognized, enlivened, and challenged by the experienced driver, who tethers that spatialized knowledge to the guidance of asphalted common sense, or the understanding of how to effectively occupy the vehicular environment of the roadscape. The life of vehicular law is enlivened through the spontaneous social interactions between drivers and paved infrastructure that generate the local roadscape. Known commonly as "rules of the road," these social interactions engender meaning through localized cultural specifics regarding spatial interactions, time for waiting on other drivers' responses, and (im)patience regarding experience with any given paved environment. The rules of the road are informally enforced approaches to interacting with the asphalt that may not be uniform across vehicular landscapes, but instead reveal the unique social character of a locale made visible in the treatment of drivers toward one another in the anonymous and temporary space of intersections. These animated negotiations of law on pavement illustrate the many ways in which law is channeled as well as challenged and contested in vehicular space. Through these negotiations, a tension of who's in charge arises and sometimes erupts. This same tension is present in jurisprudential disputes involving authority over and adherence to the rules. However, not all rules are followed; in the paved terrain, often those rules aren't even clear. Yet, regardless of law's perhaps intentional opacity, the roadscape is a space of constant flow and occasional interruption. Communication and interaction become law, as these examples will explain.

Wittgenstein reminds us that meaning is revealed through the social context of words, rather than in words themselves (Valverde 2003, 6). In this way, we can think of the social context of the vehicular built environment as one that generates meanings from the words on the signs or the painted lines on the pavement. Consider the example of the four-way stop sign. Although formal traffic laws prescribe expected behavior (such as coming to a full stop and waiting for the car on one's right to cross through the intersection), social norms dictate actual circumstances which may not be so precisely technical. In this way, the pavementality behind pavement-based interactions provides insight into how law works when motion and anonymity are involved, such as on the road. These social norms include the considerate waving to other drivers to proceed in some places (such as in relaxed rural settings), or the refusal to acknowledge the presence of other drivers by plowing through such an intersection, often without stopping. Sometimes that stop is a rolling stop and not a stop at all, but effectively a yield. Another comparable example is the flashing of headlights to communicate a message to oncoming drivers in order to alert them to danger or law enforcement waiting ahead. In these two examples, formal law serves as more of a suggestion than an enforceable infraction, and the right of way becomes a dynamic form of legality through practiced reality. Two other examples of this socio-legal dynamic response would be the yellow traffic light and the roundabout. In both of these situations, law gives us a foundation for making choices; however, these choices are ultimately individually determined, spontaneously enacted, and often without formal oversight.

When considering the road, we can see a built environment with a foundation of pavement or gravel or tracks left behind from cars passing over this terrain. This paved landscape is a feature of contemporary vehicular environments and includes our riding in cars, driving on roads, and being identified through our vehicles and vehicular associations. Roads and the rules of the road reveal the animated negotiations of law engendered through pavement-based relationships. In thinking about roads, where we travel and how we travel are both relevant factors in our vehicularized lives. Roads, and the architecture of roads provide, hinder or prevent access by the vehicular public (or those people who drive cars, buses, trucks, or scooters). A vehicularized public is a motorized public. Roads are predominantly built with cars in mind and through this construction, driving behavior is prescribed through formal law and enlivened through public interaction not only with other drivers, but with the road itself. The built environment of the roadscape is evident in the flattened linear terrain of asphalt with over-markings of white, yellow, solid, dotted lines and lanes, as well as vertical signage directing traffic flow. Roads are built for movement; however, that movement is not absolute. Possible interrupters of movements, such as stopping for hitchhikers, slowing down (a lot) for horses, tractors, or bicycles, or even oncoming ambulances (or other emergency vehicles approaching with great speed), are either directed (pull over to the side of the road and let the speeding vehicle pass) or prohibited (such as the aforementioned presence on interstates or many state highways).

The knowledge of the road is rooted in the experiential learning of drivers over time. As the road meanders through intersections and is interrupted by stop signs, traffic lights, and other embodied aspects of the roadscape, the road itself positions the driver to gain knowledge from the social aspects of interactions with the pavement involving fellow members of the driving public who co-inhabit the roadscape. Although knowledge about the road is originally sourced from driving manuals and driving lessons that initiate a driver's relationship with the vehicular environment, standards and uniform procedures are challenged in everyday vehicular interactions. In this way, the actual knowledge of driving progressively develops through the lived relationship of the driver's relationship to the pavement from behind the wheel. Like much in everyday life, legal understandings of how law should work are often massaged through social enhancement that tweak and evolve the law's hegemonic stance in what should happen on the road as the dichotomy between the learned and the lived generates new rules of the road. In other words, the vehicular positionalities of drivers on asphalt create certain legalized understandings of social relationships that carry over to the legal life of the pavement.

Through pavement, the concept and practice of territorialization is examined according to the conceptualization of the right-of-way as afforded to traffic in the roadscape. As an aspect of pavementality, the right-of-way is the asserted propertization of pavement insofar as access is claimed or given away. As a disciplining standard, the right-of-way is a practice of pavementality engineered into the governing formality of road rules and the building of road terrain and informally exercised by drivers in response to the layout of the road within the physical roadscape. Recognizing and yielding the right-of-way is a strategy of inhabiting the roadscape in which the socialization between drivers becomes visible through intentional vehicular positioning and the give and take of vehicular motion. Often, that positioning is in response to the physicality of the terrain; however, this positioning also reflects the assertion of one idea over another and tests the reaches of formal law. Whether at intersections or at four-way stops, the right of way is an application of informal law and testament to the phenomenon of pavementality.

Another way in which the social understanding of regulation contributes to culturally contextualized vehicular operation that contradicts formal driving laws is at a four-way stop sign intersection. According to formal driving instruction, drivers at a four-way stop should yield the right-of-way to the driver on the right. However, the visual cues of communication that often happen at such intersections have less to do with formal right-of-way guidelines and more to do with social recognition of what can be construed as right-of-way that is individually and fleetingly determined. Such cues may include a wave to proceed, a wave of thanks, or perhaps even a honk or rude gesture to protest the ignoring of other drivers' presence by driving ahead without acknowledging other drivers at the intersection. Visually, eye contact is essential in recognizing both legal and not-so-legal exercising as well as passing on of the right-of-way. Through visual cues and communication, we can visualize culturally respondent frameworks of how regulation works. The law of the intersection with the four-way stop sign is to look, communicate with other drivers present, and to proceed carefully without getting hit, despite what the manuals suggest as formal right-of-way procedures. For example, in Hawai'i, respect for other drivers is referred to on state-funded signage as *driving with aloha* (Marusek 2016). *Driving with aloha* is a standard of driver behavior that reflects the social nuances of a culture that is warm and welcoming. *Driving with aloha* reflects cultural interactions that are respectful, cautious, unassuming, relaxed, and generous. Localized standards of social behavior are transmitted to the vehicular environment. Happy honking only, slowing down to let drivers cut into the queue, slowing down in general, and allowing pedestrians to cross are examples of *driving with aloha*. Being respectful of other drivers at an intersection with a four-way stop sign is also an example of *driving with aloha*. As a cultural practice, *driving with aloha* is officially pronounced by Hawai'i Governor David Ige, who proclaims, in the Hawai'i State Driver's Manual (n.d., 3), "I encourage you to show your 'aloha spirit' when you drive. Be patient, courteous and watch the road at all times".

Materially, culture can be visualized through a legal lens of order and, likewise, as resistance to that order. In other words, expectations of behavior and the understandings as well as challenges to those expectations provide material manifestations of how law works in everyday life. Material manifestations of law in everyday life reference those aspects of culture that develop socio-legal understandings of and engagement with what is understood to be law (Brigham 2009). This understanding may be construed and critiqued as normative, insofar as cultural frameworks can themselves be normative, yet voluntary as expectations and associations rather than as imperatives. It is this understanding that constructs a sense of recognition that lends support to observational data as one aspect of a visual legal methodology. In this sense, observational data is normative through its recognition, but contested because of its uniformity and hegemonic presence through a variety of responses that can be observed and subsequently observed as data. This resistance reveals the normative, while also countering the culturally expected normative reception of law through cultural expectations of understanding and compliance. While we may understand the concept of the right-of-way and often act upon it, we also ignore it and either proceed out of turn or allow another driver to proceed out of turn or simply honk our horn and drive on through the intersection. Similarly, we may see flashing headlights but miss the meaning in the cue. In this way, law is culturally present and often, but not always, recognized and responded to as a primary source of regulation.

Another example of pavementality is the American yellow light (Marusek 2014). Each driver must exercise her own personal and contextualized judgment concerning the uniqueness of each intersectional transaction. In Hawai'i, as in many states, the law is silent about which is better: either to speed up or to slow down. The law leaves it up to each driver to make the most appropriate and safest decision in each fleeting momentary situation. Again, law provides a guideline that becomes a suggestion but not fact. Contextualizing law through individualized circumstances and interpretations may in fact be something that sustains law's ability to influence through the fluidity of contextual application. Despite this capriciousness, however, law is a colonizing force that compels action. Foucault reminds us that despite our various interpretations of law and its contextualized applications, the very existence, if not understanding, of order via guidelines initiated by the state, is the reification of formal governance and state power through our willing performance as well as our active resistance to it. The built vehicular environment is based on foundations and interactions with the ubiquitous use of asphalt as legal medium.

This experiential knowledge that is developed through vehicular positionality is the individual response to a yellow light, either to slow down or speed through before the light turns to red. That decision is predicated upon a driver's fleeting judgment of whether or not the intersection is safe to speed through or if it's more appropriate in that instance to slow down and stop for the red light. The visual cues concerning social communication about the legal activity of driving are an aspect of observational data in which individual experience regarding such activity is understood within a cultural framework that generates law and legal understanding through the recognitions and responses within everyday occurrences that challenge formal legal frameworks (such as in driving manuals). Observational data is therefore data that is both subjectively experienced and interpreted and can characterize culture in all of its ubiquitous banality. While "culture" is a multivariable term that means a variety of different things, the relationship between law and cultures can be seen through daily interactions that invoke legality within a cultural framework of normativity. The relationship between law and culture is constitutive insofar as each informs the other to generate as well as contest what law is and where it comes from. By observing, analyzing, and contextualizing everyday cultural interactions, law can be witnessed as responses to regulation exemplified in ordinary ways that illuminate the normative paradigm of order, authority, and engagement. Seeing law is to visualize regulation. Seeing and digesting, recognizing and responding, visual approaches to cultural normativity provides insight into everyday normative exchanges that illuminate legality.

The added element of light in the vehicular environment can be a welcome respite from the night-time darkness or thick fog. Light can come in the form of reflectors on the pavement that designate the edges of the pavement or outline of the lane. Light can also come in the form of overhead streetlamps that diffuse light above the pavement using gases such as argon or sodium vapor. Light can also come from occupants of the vehicular environment as a car's headlights. While the politics of the visual insofar as streetlamps can be costly and do not present on all roadscapes to illuminate the roadscape at night or during inclement weather, sources of light on the road can be funded by public monies; however, sources of light that exist on the front of cars as headlights can be considered to be a free public resource where streetlamps are not present. Providing the necessary illumination of a darkened roadway, vehicular headlights act as the eyes of a car as they effectively see where on the roadscape it is safe to travel. What lies ahead on the roadscape is an unknown despite the possible and even probable likelihood that other cars, possibly wild animals, and even law enforcement may be ahead.

Reflectors depend upon a car's headlight as the source of light that can be reflected for lighting purposes. Reflectors can be on signs or embedded on the pavement itself. Reflectors only reflect and do not independently generate light. Rather than a constant stream of light, sometimes a car's headlights will flash in intentional ways. Interpreting the meaning of oncoming headlights that flash is an element of the politics of the visual on the roadscape. The politics of the visual recognizes the priority of sight for the sighted in terms of seeing the landscape. In her critique of videography, Dvora Yanow (2014, 682) reminds us that "through socialization or training, we learn to interpret visual materials just as we do textual ones." The textual elements of light on the roadscape can be interpreted as not only the presence of another vehicle, but also as possible communication between drivers in ways similar to taps and beeps of Morse code. As Yanow (2014, 682) quotes Tim Pachirat, "The visual is not some unmediated mode of communication that escapes the. . .hermeneutics that we apply to texts." In the vehicular environment, the road socializes us to interpret the flashing of an oncoming car's headlights to mean something. As a hermeneutic of vehicular communication, flashing headlights represent a message from one driver to another on the roadscape: *Look out! Something ahead needs immediate attention!*

Presumably, the flashing is meant to convey a message from one driver to another. Such visual cues that are pavement-dependent depict the road as a cultural habitat of law as vehicle drivers are licensed according to legal knowledge of driving. However, the culture of driving is one that challenges the formality of driving-based law as the experience of driving is often more culturally than legally determined. Driving incorporates many forms of vehicular regulation that are obeyed, challenged, even simply ignored through the frequency of driving. Simply stated, driving doesn't always happen according to the rules we learn in driving manuals. Regulation on the road is often communicated through drivers' understandings of vehicular interactions that are driver-dependent. An example of this contextualization of vehicular operator normativity is the flashing of headlights, understood to mean that one driver flashes his/her headlights as a signal to oncoming drivers that special attention should be paid to what the initial driver just passed and what oncoming drivers will soon confront. Such flashing can warn of a disturbance in the road, a vehicle in distress, an approaching emergency vehicle, or simply (and perhaps more often than not) law enforcement policing the speed limit. This last possibility of flashing acts as a social warning between drivers to slow down in order to avoid a speeding ticket (and outsmart the intended speed trap). In this latter case, the flashing headlights act as visual cues of impending regulation that are socially communicated and culturally recognized as a response to law's presence on the roadway. While fleeting in occurrence and devoid of the formal instruction found in driver manuals, this type of cultural interaction conveys a meaning about law regarding law enforcement's ability to enforce speed limits. The flashing of headlights was recently determined to be constitutionally protected speech under the First Amendment despite law enforcement's claim that such flashing inhibited police abilities.[5] In this way, the visual message of flashing headlights is a signal that law is present. It is a visual cue about regulation that culturally employs normative understandings of driver behavior but also the understanding that nobody wants a speeding ticket. In this way, regulation is imperfect, as the act of flashing headlights contests the authority of the stealth used by law enforcement officers lying in wait for speeding drivers. The normative response to law here is premised upon the visual recognition of drivers' signals to one another as informative exchanges that are, through this recent court decision, legal forms of speech.

While the technology of the headlight is to light the path of a car, even if overhead streetlamps light up the roadscape, such technology also illuminates how drivers digest the laws of the roadscape. Such a conflation of technology with practiced meaning is what Haridimos Tsoukas (1997) might consider to be a paradox of the information society as persistent in the vehicular environment. In his article "The Tyranny of Light," Tsoukas (1997, 827) warns against knowledge that is "understood as information, that is consisting of objectified, commodified, abstract, decontextualized representations." Yet, the paradox of flashing headlights as objectifiable knowledge in the context of the vehicular environment is legally protected as a form of speech to warn against the oncoming presence of law enforcement. In this way, the contextualized representation of resistance to law that is in the form of a police radar gun that monitors speeding in a covert way on the roadscape, is in fact a form of knowledge that is unique to the roadscape. Such communication is as Tsoukas (1997, 837) articulates that "what, however, is underestimated in exercises of this kind is the constitutive"; the legal protection of flashing headlights as a protected form of speech is the constitutive dimension of the communication inherent to a roadscape of traveling vehicles and patrolling law enforcement. Of course, having acquired the knowledge of what flashing headlights might mean is the foundation for such communication.

Street Names

Similar in scope to the pavementality exercised through the flashing of lights or the waves at the four-way stop intersection, the pavementality of using the naming of streets as a source of public memory enlivens the present through the past. The names of people and of places give rise to contemporary understandings of place through the street name. The naming of streets is a jurisdictional statement of the history and culture of a place through the asphalted reference to concepts, people, and use of language. Whether as the ubiquitous Main Street associated with Small Town USA or as more contextualized and specific references to place (Pili 2018), the common reference to place that a street name conveys reveals yet another application of pavementality. Popular memory is inscribed through street names. Additionally, the acculturation of place can be characterized through the names of streets. Augé (1995, 66) notes that "Roads and crossroads in France tend to become 'monuments' (in the sense of testimonies and reminders) when the names they have been given immerse them in history." As history changes, the street names change too, both in France and

Figure 2.2 Kinoole Street in Hilo, Hawai'i

elsewhere. Memory is shaped by the public reference to place. In this way, the street name is the naming of territory and jurisdictional reflection in this final exercise of pavementality. The asphalted pavement is often named to remember a person or event in history that is vital to a constructed understanding of public memory.

In his research on Kinoole Street in Hilo, Hawai'i, Kamaka Pili (2018) finds that this central street in the second largest city in the State of Hawai'i was actually originally named Pitman Street, named "after a Benjamin Pitman, a Massachusetts businessman who married Kino'oleliliha, High Chiefess of the Kingdom of Hawai'i." During the mid-1800s, this union was a strategic marriage between a businessman and Ali'i (Hawaiian royalty) that ultimately resulted in plantations, ranches, banks, and other business establishments throughout the state. Currently, this street is renamed as Kino'ole Street to reflect and honor the High Chiefess, Kino'oleliliha, although, as Figure 2.2 shows, the Hawaiian punctuation separating Kino and ole with the use of an 'okina, or glottal stop, is not reflected on the contemporary street sign of Kinoole Street. Yet, even as the street sign lacks the formally correct punctuation, the word is locally pronounced as if it did have it.

In the localized context of Hawai'i, street names are a method of re-propertizing the roadscape through efforts to characterize place once again through the intentional renaissance and repositioning of the Hawaiian language as culturally framing. The cultural importance of having street names in the Hawaiian language is a statement of propertizing Hawai'i's roadscape in words that are themselves Hawaiian for the purpose of re-making this place as Hawaiian. In this way, the naming of the street is the propertizing of the paved for the politicizing of the paved terrain. While some may ask, *What's in a name?* the importance of keeping a language, a culture, and a history alive happens in Hawai'i through the naming of streets. In Hawai'i, street names have evolved from the names of American businessmen who previously overthrew the Hawaiian monarchy (Herman 1999) to words and names from the Hawaiian language that are descriptive of a particular place. Although this change is a statement of changing political power, the street with a name is nonetheless indicative of American hegemony as "embedded in the place-name code" (Herman 1999, 77). This hegemonic code is indicative of the "shift of human-environment discourses and their political-economic contexts towards a capitalist understanding of space that served Western (*haole*) interests" (Herman 1999, 77). In a statement reflecting local resistance to a contested American dominance in this formerly thriving independent monarchal republic, Dr. Lilikalā Kame'eleihiwa of the University of Hawai'i Mānoa states, "They're lucky Hawaiians don't rise up and burn the street sign" (Herman 1999, 77). The street sign and its evolution as a naming site reveal an understanding of pavementality that positions memorialization against everyday banality.

Street names reveal the workings of power which may seek to achieve a revision of the normative *logos* insofar as knowing where one is based upon the surrounding naming of pavement. Popular references to places are a function of determining directions as well as thinking of place in an intentional way (Bradley 2018) As a way to re-intentionalize the semiotics of street names as hegemonically English words and names that served as street names in Hawai'i, the 1974 Hawai'i State Legislature created the Hawai'i State Board on Geographic Names to recreate the standards for which place names evolved in Act 50, Hawai'i Revised Statutes.[6] According to Act 50, this Board has been tasked with the following responsibility:

> The board shall designate the official names and spellings of geographic features in Hawaii and provide for circulation thereof to the appropriate state and other agencies. In its deliberations, the board shall solicit and consider the advice and recommendations of the appropriate county government officials, and, should the board desire, other knowledgeable persons.

Ultimately, the Board submits their findings to the national U.S. Board on Geographic Names. The purpose of the Board is to ensure the correct names and spelling from Pukui, Elbert, and Mookini's *Place Names of Hawaii* (1976), as well as from local Hawaiian *kupuna* (elders) with extensive knowledge of the Hawaiian language. According to the Board, the *Guidelines for Hawaiian Geographic Names*[7] notes that the Board is to

> assure uniformity in the use and spelling of the names of geographic features within the State. . . [in order that] the standardized spelling of geographic names allows the public to communicate unambiguously about places, reducing the potential for confusion.

Act 50 was in response to the attempt of Americans to criminalize the speaking of the Hawaiian Language while Hawai'i was a U.S. territory. Through the 1970s Hawaiian Language Renaissance and the decades since, the street names in the Hawaiian language that appear throughout the Hawaiian roadscapes remind the public of where they are. However, the practice of street names in an American state in a language other than English enlivens the Hawai'i State Constitution of 1978 in which Hawaiian and English are the two official state languages. Therefore, the history of the Hawaiian roadscape, made visible through the legal semiotic of the street name, is the political reminder that the present State of Hawai'i was formerly a kingdom overthrown by the United States at the end of the 19th century.

In terms of pavementality, street names are a vital source of public history. Gwilym Lucas Eades (2017, 62) describes the "neurogeography of names" and the "mimetics of place" insofar as "Names refer and are referred to: names are both reference and referent, in a complex interplay of inscription, performance, embodiment, and transmission." Eades (2017, 62) details the "meme" as the idea that "intergenerational spatial knowledge constructs are passed along from generation to generation through performances, utterances, and inscriptions of place names." In Hawai'i, that intergenerational knowledge of place was interrupted with American territorialization and eventual statehood that threatened not only the indigenous culture but banned the speaking and teaching of the Hawaiian language. However, through the efforts of the Hawai'i State Board on Geographic Names and other similar efforts,[8] the Hawaiian lineage of place is making a comeback in ways that recognize Hawai'i through the Hawaiian language, spelling, and naming. In this way, the pavementality of street names in Hawai'i has a rich jurisdictional history with a political reclaiming of indigenous presence through the banality of the vehicular landscape.[9] The public understanding of place in Hawaii becomes increasingly more indigenously Hawaiian, as the recent renaming of Fissure 8 to *Ahu'ailā'au* perpetuates (Pili 2021). Through the presence or absence of proper punctuation, however, the street name of a street in Hawaiian may still be anglicized through the limited space afforded by the physical dimensions of the street sign and the omittance of Hawaiian punctuation, such as the 'okina or kahako.

To conclude, pavementality is the cultural practice of using pavement for purposes of communication, governance through identity, and the public engagement with place. Whether through highway adoption programs, the rules of the road that informally animate formal vehicular frameworks, or the naming of streets, pavement is a source of political, cultural, and social definition in which roads themselves invigorate the pavement-based semiotic interactions between people, place, and asphalt.

Notes

1 *KKK v. Arkansas State Highway & Transportation Department* (807 F. Supp. 1427 (W.D. Ark. 1992).

2 *Texas v. KKK*, 58 F. 3d 1075 (5th Cir. 1995).

3 *Cuffley v. Mickes*, No. 4:97CV2110-SNL, 1999WL 216439 (E.D. Mo. April 13, 1999).

4 *State of Georgia Et Al. v. International Keystone Knights of The Ku Klux Klan, Inc.* S16A0367 (July 5, 2016).

5 *Elli v. City of Ellisville* [E.D. Mo. February 3, 2014].

6 www.capitol.hawaii.gov/hrscurrent/Vol01_Ch0001-0042F/HRS0004E/HRS_0004E-0003.htm.
7 https://files.hawaii.gov/dbedt/op/gis/bgn/Guidelines_for_Hawaiian_Geographic_Names_v1.1.pdf.
8 See further the project "Mapping Puna Ahapua'a" from Kaylyn Ells-Ho'okano and Drew Kapp found at the Spatial Data Analysis and Visualization Labs at the University of Hawai'i Hilo: http://spatial.uhh.hawaii.edu/current%20research.htm.
9 See further the street names for the subdivision Hawaiian Paradise Park in the Puna District of Hawai'i Island: www.hppoa.net/roads-information/street-names/.

Reference List

Augé, Marc. 1995. *Non-Places: An Introduction to an Anthropology of Supermodernity*. Translated by John Howe. London: Verso.

Blomley, Nicholas. 2011. *Rights of Passage: Sidewalks and the Regulation of Public Flow*. New York: Routledge.

Bradley, Rachel Ross. 2018. "How Honolulu Gets Its Street Names and Neighborhood Themes." *Honolulu*, September 4, 2018. Accessed March 11, 2022. www.honolulumagazine.com/how-honolulu-gets-its-street-names-and-neighborhood-themes/.

Brigham, John. 2009. *Material Law: A Jurisprudence of What's Real*. Philadelphia: Temple University Press.

Clark, J. Don. 1989. "Adopt-a-Highway: A New Source of Pride for Americans." *Transportation Builder* 1 (1): 14–16.

Dorsett, Shaunnagh, and Shaun McVeigh. 2012. *Jurisdiction*. New York: Routledge.

Eades, Gwilym Lucas. 2017. *The Geography of Names: Indigenous to Post-Foundational*. New York: Routledge.

Eschner, Kat. 2017. "Two States Have Gone to Court to Keep the KKK From Adopting a Highway." *Smithsonian Magazine*, March 9, 2017. Accessed March 11, 2022. www.smithsonianmag.com/smart-news/brief-political-history-adopt-highway-program-180962365/.

Grinberg, Emanuella. 2016. "KKK Wins Adopt-a-Highway Ruling in Georgia High Court." *CNN*, July 6, 2016. Accessed March 11, 2022. www.cnn.com/2016/07/05/us/georgia-kkk-adopt-a-highway-lawsuit/index.html.

Gudis, Catherine. 2004. *Buyways: Billboards, Automobiles, and the American Landscape*. New York: Routledge.

Hawaii Driver's Manual. n.d. Accessed March 11, 2022. https://hidot.hawaii.gov/highways/files/2019/03/mvso-11272-Hawaii-Drivers-Manual-r3-LR-10-24-18.pdf

Herman, R. D. K. 1999. "The Aloha State: Place Names and the Anti-Conquest of Hawai'i." *Annals of the American Association of Geographers* 89 (1): 76–102.

Ingold, Tim. 2015. *The Life of Lines*. New York: Routledge

Ingold, Tim. 2016. *Lines*. New York: Routledge.

Loukaitou-Sideris, Anastasia, and Renia Ehrenfeucht. 2009. *Sidewalks: Conflict and Negotiation over Public Space*. Cambridge: MIT Press.

Marusek, Sarah. 2014. "Visual Jurisprudence of the American Yellow Traffic Light." *International Journal for the Semiotics of Law* 27 (1): 183–91.

————. 2016. "The Aloha Paradox: Law and Culture in Hawai'i." *Space and Polity* 21 (1): 108–22.

Mohr, Richard, and Nadirsyah Hosen. 2017. "Everyday Jurisprudence in Urban Australia: Negotiating the Space of Legal Performances." In *Street-Level Sovereignty: The Intersection of Space and Law*, 67–89. Lanham, MD: Lexington.

Montgomery, Suzanne Stone. 1999. "When the Klan Adopts-a-Highway: The Weaknesses of the Public Form Doctrine Exposed." *Washington University Law Review* 77 (2): 557–83.

Morton, Katherine. 2016. "Hitchhiking and Missing and Murdered Indigenous Women." *The Canadian Journal of Sociology* 41 (3): 299–326.

Pili, Kamaka. 2018. "Aloha Authentic: Meaning, History of Kinoole Street." Accessed March 11, 2022. www.youtube.com/watch?v=iGFL9Uqia2I.

————. 2021. "Fissure 8 Officially Given a Hawaiian Name." *Khon2 News*, March 4, 2021. Accessed March 11, 2022. www.khon.com/local-news/fissure-8-officially-given-a-hawaiian-name/

"The Pothole." *Seinfeld* Season 8, Episode 16, originally aired February 20, 1997.

Pukui, Mary Kawena, Samuel H. Elbert, and Esther H. Mookini. 1976. *Place Names of Hawaii: Revised and Expanded Edition*. Honolulu: University of Hawai'i Press.

Tsoukas, Haridimos. 1997. "The Tyranny of Light: The Temptations and the Paradoxes of the Information Society." *Futures* 29 (9): 827–43.

Valverde, Mariana. 2003. *Law's Dream of a Common Knowledge*. Princeton: Princeton University Press.

Yanow, Dvora. 2014. "I Am Not a Camera: On Visual Politics and Method. A Response to Roy Germano." *Perspectives on Politics* 12 (3): 680–83.

3   Pavementeering

Rife with purpose, intention, and invited social engagement with the infrastructure of the paved roadway, the roadscape is a legal place animated through the fluidity of pavementeering, social discipline, and visual communication between drivers involving roadscape conditions and the process of making the paved into property. In the roadscape, the pavement is often the subject of debate of who owns what territory and how. Propertizing the pavement is a fluid process where construction, occupancy, and use serve as the basis for assertions of property. Ownership is less of a priority in this process than the declaration of spatial claim. Within the roadscape, the vehicular environment creates unique understandings of property and ownership through the contested spaces of where cars can be driven. The driveability of this space becomes a commodity of accessibility with cars on roads serving as rites of passage, literally. The flows of rightful passage (Blomley 2011) depend upon the asphalt itself as animated matter (Bennett 2010) and how the public manages that asphalt. These tensions exist at a localized level, as the roadscape is a site of locally inhabited space, even as the road itself may fall under state or national jurisdiction or mandates. Through this localization, the vehicular environment engenders an understanding, engagement with, and practice of the public through motion in vehicular space. According to Augé (1995, 49), "the idea of culture as text, which is one of the more recent manifestations of American culturalism, is already present in its entirety in the notion of localized society." As a cultural text, the roadscape takes on the qualities of a surrounding localized culture and localized sense for the distinct dimensionality of pavementeering that exists between private versus public practices of jurisdictional authority. This debate revolves around understandings of space as property, or in other words, the propertizing of the paved in the roadscape for privatized access, if not ownership. In this way, the ability to travel on the roadscape embarks a privatized sense of public engagement on the road linked

DOI: 10.4324/9781315231853-3

Figure 3.1 Pavementeering with Ahuʻailāʻau in the Distance

Figure 3.2 Ahuʻailāʻau

to access of the pavement. Moreover, that ability hinges on the contested jurisdictional frameworks of control that determine the degree to which a roadscape may be either privatized or public. The resulting territorialization of the pavement through propertization can be referred to as the pavementeering of the roadscape.

Through its construction, the roadscape is the site for connectivity in a vehicular society. As shortcuts, the roadscape connects people and places. For example, we drive through the roadscape to enjoy the view as we drive through previously (vehicularly) impassable mountains, or more simply, we drive these routes to save time by taking shorter routes through difficult terrains. As deliberate pastimes, the roadscape provides a path for leisure either through a scenic drive and/or roadtrip. As the bedrock for commuting, the roadscape provides expressways to drive from home to work or school. Yet the roadscape is also the expression for a revisited Manifest Destiny, in which the postcolonial expansion of the United States in the late twentieth century can be seen in the paving through/over indigenous lands across America.[1] With this in mind, we can consider the construction of other roads in terms of their sinister and destructive origins. Whether as highways in Poland built by forced labor from Nazi-era camps (Allen 2017) or Stalin's "Highway of Bones" Kolyma Highway in Siberia (Higgins 2020), paving a pathway for the car has come at great cost to untold numbers of people and cultures around the world.

Ahuʻailāʻau, *Formerly Fissure 8*

The first application of pavementeering is the propertizing of the pavement through jurisdictional prerogative. This prerogative was exerted by one particular landowner in the Puna district of Hawaiʻi Island following the Kīlauea eruption of 2018. By attempting to repave his driveway in an area of land that was inundated by lava and lay directly beneath the largest, most active lava cone, this local resident incurred the wrath of his neighbors. The ensuing tension involved the neighborhood group who sought to stop the repropertizing of his property through pavement, and the property rights of the homeowner who had the unfortunate luck of having a home that was directly at the site of Ahuʻailāʻau, previously referred to as Fissure 8. The jurisdictional efforts of the man's neighbors were not clear because the neighborhood and neighborhood association were a private subdivision; however, under state law, new lava is public to the extent that lava is the property of the State of Hawaiʻi. The jurisdictional complexity in this fourth application of the larger chapter's conceptualization of property and jurisdiction through the territorialization of the roadscape is indicative of this man's personal struggle to restart his life through the reclamation of his personal property against the backdrop of the public spectacle of lava.

In the summer of 2018 on the Island of Hawai'i, Kīlauea Volcano erupted within the residential subdivisions of Leilani Estates and Lanipuna Gardens. In a period of a few months, around twenty-four fissure vents opened in this volcanic rift zone in the District of Puna. Molten lava burst from the vents and covered houses and roads in subdivision neighborhoods. The eighth fissure to open, and ultimately the most active of all the vents, came to be known as Fissure 8. With lava fountains roughly two hundred feet high, the lava from Fissure 8 resulted in nearly $800 million in property damage (Associated Press 2018; Jones 2019). As the largest and most active fissure, Fissure 8 was renamed *Ahu'ailā'au* in March 2021 by the Hawai'i Board of Geographic Names (Pili 2021). According to Marques Hanalei Marzon, Chairman of the Hawai'i Board of Geographic Names, the Hawaiian name *Ahu'ailā'au* comes from *Ahu* (mound or shrine), *'Ailā'au* (fire deity who precedes the more familiar Pele, Goddess of Fire and Volcanoes), *'Ai* (to eat), and *Lā'au* (to heal, medicine) and conveys the idea of a "ancestorial guardian and deity for Puna" and "a healing element for the community" (Pili 2021). The renaming of Fissure 8 to *Ahu'ailā'au* is a message to the community of proceeding with the continuation of life after the disruption to the landscape, lives, and property of those impacted by flowing lava. As the renaming also possibly suggests, lava itself can be a material point of healing for the residents of these two subdivisions in Puna. For one resident of Leilani Estates, Sam Estes, the healing started with the process of regaining access to his residence and ornamental plant farm that had been covered by lava of *Ahu'ailā'au* (Brestovansky 2020). In mid-December 2020, Estes began to bulldoze the side of *Ahu'ailā'au* in an attempt to reclaim what had been covered by lava.

Soon the repaving of Estes' former driveway became a struggle over the development of this new land. Was this newly formed cindercone in fact new public land? Did part of it belong to Estes? Or did all of it now belong to the Leilani Community Association (LCA), the governing body of this private residential subdivision? According to Robert Golden, LCA President, the association "had told Estes in August that it would not remove road barricades at the edges of the lava fields until a thorough assessment had been done about the safety of such an action" (Brestovansky 2020). Regardless, Estes did not wait for the outcome of the assessment; he removed the barricades himself in order to start bulldozing the land and build a road on his property. The LCA was now enmeshed in a quandary involving public access and private property ownership. In the words of Golden, some Leilani residents "wanted Fissure 8 to be a park, or just a geological feature, without any human development" (Brestovansky 2020). Others were concerned that Estes' independent construction of a road "might set a precedent for other residents to cut their own potentially dangerous roads across lava on their own properties" (Brestovansky 2020). Citing "community rights" asserted by the LCA to the private land that became the geological wonder of *Ahuʻailāʻau*, Golden opted to let the local municipal government decide whether Estes' road was legitimately initiated under County building permits.

In a nod to Elinor Ostrom's (1990) idea of governing the commons where "common-pool resources" become the purview of "self-organization and self-governance," the LCA argued that *Ahuʻailāʻau* should be purchased with public monies for the purposes of preservation. In March 2021, a group from the private residential subdivision of Leilani Estates in which the 2018 Kīlauea Eruption took place argued that *Ahuʻailāʻau* was a place of natural wonder that should be available to the public. In the words of Leilani Estates resident Alice Lindahi and quoted by Nancy Cook Lauer (2021), the "preservation of the fragile features [should be] prioritized while creating educational opportunities and a nature trail for tourists to help control and channel the inevitable crowds from residential areas once the coronavirus pandemic is finished." For residents such as Lindahi to advocate the public takeover of a neighbor's property following the initial takeover of the property by Madame Pele, the Hawaiian Goddess of Fire and the Volcano, the pavementeering of a public right to nature versus private property rights comes to bear. In his work on property and entitlements, John Brigham (1990, 3) reminds us that

> even in its most basic form, property is not a material thing. In conventional terms it is the relationship between people and the thing. In more careful analysis, the definition of that relationship in law creates the thing. . . property is a legal construction.

Brigham argues that property should be a democratic construction, as property is based in a relationship between people and things that is mediated, even constructed by law. This insight into the conceptualization of what propertization entails provides keen insight into the struggle over Estes' ability to build a road on his property. Ultimately, the County of Hawaiʻi determined that no permits for building this road were needed, as the repaving of Estes' former driveway did not require a permit because the road itself did not meet the threshold requiring a grading permit; the grade of the road would not affect neighboring properties in terms of drainage (Brestovansky 2021). In considering the schism that erupts between neighbors, Stuart Scheingold's (2004) dichotomy between the politics of rights and the myth of rights is demonstrated by Estes's own pavementeering that this was his land to reclaim through the grading of the soil. Because the road is "not a county road" (Brestovansky 2021), it's unclear whether the road is owned by the Leilani Estates subdivision or Estes. Interestingly, though, land that extends the existing shoreline through lava from a volcanic eruption becomes the property of the State of Hawai'i.[2] However, it is less clear what happens if private property is covered rather than extended through the inundation of lava, such as in Estes' case. The issue of pavementeering arising from Estes' attempt to repave his driveway invokes larger issues of mobility, access, and the public usage of private property in cases of natural change, such as new land arising from a lava flow.

Mauna Kea Access Road

In a second approach to pavementeering, we can consider the physicality of access and its restriction via the road in recent contests involving the construction of a new telescope on the summit of Mauna Kea on Hawai'i Island. In late May 2016 on the slopes of Mauna Kea, large rocks were found blocking the primary access road. These rocks had been organized horizontally on the downhill slope of the road in the middle of a sharp, right-hand corner (Khon2 2016) that was unable to be seen by those driving down the mountain. Witnessed by some as well as a recording video camera, the rocks were linked to an unknown individual seen carrying a large backpack.

The placement of the rocks is a not a new occurrence, as rocks had been placed some months earlier in a similar manner on Mauna Kea Access Road, yet in a chaotic dispersal of rocks randomly spread across the road. At other times and during this same period, the rocks were intentionally gathered and purposively arranged into an 'ahu, or Hawaiian altar. During the spring of 2015 and 2016, Mauna Kea Access Road was the site of political unrest involving the pending construction of the internationally managed and funded Thirty Meter Telescope. At nearly 14,000 feet and remotely positioned in the Pacific Ocean without light pollution or atmospheric distractions, Mauna Kea is known as the world's premier site for astronomy and an optimal site to build the world's largest and most sophisticated telescope. The Thirty Meter Telescope (henceforth referred to as TMT) is an international venture involving the United States and a team of partners from scientific organizations around the world, including India, China, Japan, Canada, and others. Those partnering to build the TMT would join a number of established U.S. and international observatories that have been located on the mountain's summit since 1967. However, in addition to being a perfect site for astronomy, Mauna Kea, also known as Mauna O Wakea, is the sacred home for many Native Hawaiians. Activist groups, many of whom were located on the U.S. mainland and on neighboring Hawaiian Islands, sought to protect the mountain from construction by blocking access to the summit. These rocks and their placement on the road are associated with this protest, as the construction of this particular telescope became a source of political tension during the spring and summer months of 2015, 2016, and again in 2019. During this time, construction activities ceased as many protestors camped, engaged in nonviolent sit-ins, and, as the pictures show, barricaded the road with large boulders to literally stop those traversing the road, of which the lower half is asphalt and the upper half is gravel. Impeding traffic was the initial approach taken by protestors to halt construction, actions which were later challenged by the Hawai'i Supreme Court's support for the project (Hurley 2018) but not implemented by Governor David Ige due to protest on the lower road in 2019 (Associated Press 2019).

The road up to the summit where the observatories are located was the site of the protest. Paved up to the area of the Visitor's Center at roughly 9000 feet, the road continues for another six miles as gravel and is quite steep. This road, Mauna Kea Access Road, a site of political resistance, became a vital site for protest: in 2015, the road past the Visitor's Center and in 2019, the entry of the road from the Daniel K. Inouye Highway, also known as Saddle Road.

As places for travel, usually by vehicular traffic, roads are sites of intentional movement and the facilitation of movement from place to place. Access is an expectation of roads in which the unfettered ability to traverse the road is presumed. As these photos show, obstacles were placed in such a way as to interrupt that flow. The road itself was viewed as a site of postcolonial resistance, as this paved terrain reflected a venue to express culture's complex relationship with law. As a site of legal materiality in which movement serves as jurisprudential foundation, the road, its construction, its usage, and its interrupted fluidity provide a context for envisioning the aesthetics and spatiality of law through motion. In considering the discursive construction of movement versus non-movement, we can see that on the mountain, the road conveys movement but also invites the act of resistance to that movement.

It is the flow of traffic that the rocks placed on Mauna Kea Access Road were meant to interrupt. This interruption was a political statement, a method of invoking law through direct and informal methods (i.e., no stop signs or official police barriers were erected). The interruption was premised on interrupting the flow happening in this place. The place and the road accessing this place were the site of controversy. However, politically, the identities of those drivers may have been relevant and less so anonymous, as the expectation might have been directed to those working on the summit at the telescopes or those hoping to build the TMT (as was the original reason for changing the accessibility of the roadway through boulders that would keep construction equipment from proceeding (and accessing the summit to build)). Mauna Kea Access Road is a public road insofar as it is open to the public, funded through public means, and is publicly traversed. It was built and is still maintained by the University of Hawai'i. However, the purpose behind travel on this public road during the months of protest reveals more about the privatized nature of roads than simply public funding of pavement and associated accessibility.

Valverde (2003) refers to the phenomenon of everyday governance as "law's dream of a common knowledge" in which the sense about law, from law's perspective, would be generally understood. On Mauna Kea, common knowledge translates to the road as a linear avenue of access. This road is a designated site of ordering as well as resistance to the expectation of unencumbered fluid movement and travel up and down the mountain. The road compels us to use it, as vehicles that travel to the summit drive on, rather than off, the road. Driving off-road is seen as dangerous, impractical because of the rocks, and culturally disrespectful. It is through this association of the road and accessibility that the road becomes a site of resistance, as the rocks placed strategically to disrupt the flow of traffic reveal. Drawing upon Valverde, we can see evidence in both cases that the road is commonly understood to be a place for cars and car travel. Interestingly, this ordering of both traffic flow as well as protest on the pavement (that turns into gravel) reveal that law in vehicular environments, such as Mauna Kea Access Road, is understood as linear through boundaries that appear as the road's shoulders. The rocks, if placed off to the road's shoulder, would lack the weight (literally) that they had when placed directly on the road. It is socially understood that vehicles are blocked by such rocks; however, legally, rocks in themselves are not illegal, nor are they violent when placed as they were despite their possible outcome. It is through Valverde's nuanced reading of how law works that we conflate presumably violent intention with rock placement, whether that placement is linear or scattered. In this way, the common knowledge about law is such that anonymously placed rocks on a road traveled upon by TMT construction was a way to use law for resistance purposes, as nothing overtly illegal transpired. Only through the nuance of this act of resistance can we further shed light on the road as a form of colony, particularly if we consider the construction of a road up to the summit of a sacred mountain itself an act of violence. However, the organization of the rocks into an 'ahu reveals a bit more space for dialogue, as the constructed altar does not block the entire road but conveys a sense of permanence rather than just interruption. The road is then a site of legal materiality on which a variety of uses are engendered through the road's construction and travel: travel for astronomers, travel for sunrise-seeking tourists, travel for those traveling to the summit for sacred reasons. Each of these is the outcome of a legally built, publicly accessible road up the mountain.

The protests returned in July 2019 as construction was scheduled to begin for work on the Thirty Meter Telescope (TMT). The state of Hawai'i under Governor David Ige, the Hawai'i County Civil Defense, Hawai'i National Guard (unarmed), Hawai'i County Police Department, Division of Land and Natural Resources officers, the Department of Transportation, and other state agencies (Conservation) met with hundreds of protestors on the site of the Mauna Kea Access Road at the site of the intersection with Saddle Road. Protest was centered at this intersection to prevent vehicular access up the mountain and to block construction equipment. The physical dynamics of the road involve the concrete barriers, the protestors' central location, Pu'uhonua o Pu'uhuluhulu, across the intersection, the presence of law enforcement from various jurisdictions (County, State, and National Guard), the presence of heavy construction equipment that fills the road (the equipment was quite wide on this otherwise narrow two-lane road with little or no shoulder), and the protestors tied to the cattle grate in the direct path of any oncoming vehicles.

Paved in 1964, Mauna Kea Access Road is land that is owned by the State of Hawai'i and managed by the Office of Maunakea Management through the University of Hawai'i (Mauna Kea Science Reserve Master Plan n.d.). In congruence with Lefebvre's (1991) work on spatiality, David Delaney's (2010, 34) contextualization of everyday life through "nomospheric imaginaries, performativities, and spatialities vis-à-vis the workings of power" further reminds us of De Certeau's (1984) assertion that the construction of place is an outgrowth of the ordinary. Drawing further upon Delaney, Mauna Kea Access Road is enlivened as a nomosphere with multiple interpretations. As a mountain sacred to Native Hawaiians and also as a mountain desired by global astronomy, Mauna Kea's public identity is layered in complexity that may not always need to be in competition. There isn't just one public, as the rocks show. Travel by 'the public' is multilayered – are these drivers tourists, scientists, locals, or those practicing religious worship? However, access and the impediments used to hinder access may be ways that the public is categorized through presumptions of movement, or in this case, interruptions thereof. The public interest in the mountain may in fact be privatized by those off-island and away from the observatories, Hawaiian culture on the Big Island, and ensuing relationship to the mountain by the local community since the late 1960s. The travel obstructed by rocks for the initiation of construction on the TMT may have been privatized by voices external to this nuanced and already engaged group comprised of multiple communities. This changing association with usage propels the rocks to take on particular meaning. As mentioned, this meaning is often overlapping and complex, as illustrated by the approach asserted by 'Imiloa Astronomy Center in Hilo. Here, Hawaiian knowledge of the skies through navigation and wayfinding is linked with contemporary and international frameworks of scientific technologies about the same skies.

Quite often, the roadscape becomes a site of marginalization, as the transience of the roadway teamed with the intent inherent to the thoroughfare reveals struggles for power, definition, and agency. Through the cold, seemingly neutral space of the asphalted landscape, the tension of a road's construction and usage come to the forefront. The contested colonization of the roadscape involves the building of the road, its purpose, and its usage toward a particular purpose. Moreover, the solidity of the asphalt as roadway on the earthen foundation of soil beneath the pavement is a metaphor for the solidity of power, or more specifically, power that has captured the terrain. Through the physical presence of the road, the manifestation of power in the roadscape is represented by the asphalt itself, with the intended purpose for the road now carved into the landscape. Hence, the roadscape of contested colonization is generated through the tension over place and its occupancy. Whether the road is in the process of becoming, being built, or having been built, the ensuing roadscape is a larger dynamic of positionality in which the marginalized seem to be on less-solid ground than that of the dominant paving authority. Therefore, in this type of roadscape, the purpose of the road, its construction, and its usage each play a significant role in the contestation of colonizing forces. These forces may be in the form of access to the terrain in order to pave it, to occupy it, or transgress its terrain as occupied space through which a road is paved. The colonized roadscape is a tangible marker of power and place, of people, and of progress. In this sense, progress may be future benefit, but it may also be, literally, the movement forward.

In ordinary transient situations involving vehicular access and travel, law is materially visible as a manifestation of everyday life that gives it shape and meaning. In this way, the construction of roadways, their usage by a vehicular public, and their material deterioration over time provide an interesting jurisprudential metaphor of law itself in which the process of legality follows a similar trajectory of construction, usage, deterioration, and repair. Furthermore, the contested building and usage of roads engenders frameworks of resistance to law's normative presence as vehicular hegemony. Through the building of *ahu* (stone altars) on the road accessing the summit of Mauna Kea on Hawai'i Island to hinder telescope construction and serve as sacred reminders of place, roads are sites of colony as well as resistance. Colony often becomes the legal status quo, with resistance to this status quo as the accompanying challenge. The true challenge, however, comes in questioning the status quo nature of the status quo as well as the associated polarity between colony and resistance in which astronomy, when presented as 'Imiloa does, is not the enemy. Interestingly, the road to 'Imiloa is not strewn with rocks, but instead borders gardens that celebrate endemic flora and fauna while providing vehicular access to this conflated site of multiple identities and perspectives.

The Pothole

The roadscape is a site in which the legal mandate of road construction of usage exemplifies the jurisdictional purview of paved land. Contests over the land via the road engender an aspect of the colonial roadscape that is steeped in tension involving questions of place and rightful occupancy. Law's presence in this type of roadscape is debated as representing the larger public good or the rights of the few. Embodied within the paving of the road is the contestation in response to a variety of colonizing forms of governance. The presence of the road and the act of driving on the road is contested. But also, what happens on the road is contested. In this way, the road is a metaphor for contested assertions of power by government that become tangible in the form of a paved thruway.

As we drive down the road, we expect the surface to be smooth and free from clutter. Whether cluttered intentionally as in the previous example or pitted through the effects of weather, the surface of the road is a framework to witness pavementeering. Potholes are the pitting of asphalt that results in the deterioration of the smooth surface. In the rain and snow of the Pacific Northwest, perpetual potholes plague the roads of Portland, Oregon. In a light-hearted approach to potholes, Portland's Voodoo Donuts has taken an innovative approach to filling the holes: fill the pothole with donuts that will pack down and solidify when driven over. Yet in a more serious sense, potholes serve as legal metaphor representing law's relationship to culture, insofar as the presence of a pothole and accompanying absence of a smooth road results in a critique of irresponsive governance. In Western society, it is normative to drive straight lines on paved roads that are smooth and do not require the otherwise careful navigation around existent potholes. Drawing from Tim Ingold 's work (2015, 2016), we can see that in Western societies, straight lines are everywhere and through their ubiquity, emerge as semiotics of modernity.

In this sense, the standards of pavement surface would be smooth to the point of being mundane with potholes responsibly patched and the asphalt unbroken.

While we don't typically use flattened donuts to fix potholes, we do rely on the reliable reaction of municipal government to serve as the paver of smooth roads and fixer of potholes. It is the cultural dependency on law that expects government to remedy our pothole problems, a tyranny of standards in which smooth triumphs over rough prevails. To echo Emma Goldman in her speech to the Foyle's Twenty-Ninth Literary Luncheon at Grosvenor House in London on March 1, 1933, "Nowadays most people believe that the stronger the Government the greater the success of society will be" (Goldman 1933). In the case of potholes, a strong government is a government that responds to potholes. Yet even a strong government is limited by external factors, such as a changing climate, an enlivened and dynamic landscape, and unforeseen economic instabilities. As the City of Portland Bureau of Transportation reminds the public, pothole repair is "weather dependent and crews are sometimes diverted to emergencies such as landslides" (PBOT n.d.).

Even as potholes usually get fixed, ignoring potholes can lead to anarchy, as literally the absence of government can be witnessed in the ignored and unfilled pothole. In this way, law, as well as lawlessness, are visible on the paved street with the presence or absence of potholes framing this legal landscape (Metcalfe 2017). If by filling potholes the government is promoting a tyranny of standards to the extent that we normatively expect straight-line, smooth, routine vehicular terrains without the need to navigate around potholes, we can further consider the baseline jurisprudential framework of what law considers to be "reasonable" against the notion of the tyranny of standards. Through Goldman, Ingold, and others, the status quo of what's reasonable or not according to societal norms is challenged by government response, expectations and frameworks of vehicular mobility, and standards of smoothness within the socio-legal context of reasonableness in the vehicular environment involving the legal narratives of potholes, climate change, and governmental response in American society that teeters on anarchy if the potholes go unfilled.

Portland, like many cities and municipalities across the United States, uses public awareness of the roads to diagnose problematic potholes. Particularly prone to potholes due to freeze/thaw cycles in the rainy, wintry climate of the Pacific Northwest, Portland fills more than 8000 potholes each year on its 4700 miles of publicly-maintained city streets (PBOT n.d.). The Portland Bureau of Transportation (PBOT) recognizes a pothole as having a life cycle which is otherwise smooth asphalt impacted by inclement weather. As the surface of the road becomes cracked, rainwater seeps into the damaged asphalt (generally an amalgamate of rock, gravel, and sand). As cars and other vehicles drive over the cracked asphalt, the weight of the vehicles further expands the crack by causing voids in the asphalt in a process called pumping (PBOT n.d.). Tires that continue to drive over the compromised area of asphalt further erode the layers of asphalt and soil. The result of missing chunks and fine particles of asphalt that are knocked loose by passing vehicles is known as a pothole. The pothole is a manmade hole in the asphalt, as opposed to the naturally-caused hole in the road otherwise known as a sinkhole. Sinkholes are holes that result from emptied-out pockets in the earth that were previously filled (often by water in underground aquifers) below the road's surface. Because the foundational support for the roadway is no longer there, the surface gives way often to stunningly round circular holes known as sinkholes. Sinkholes are much larger than potholes. And lastly, a delamination, which is neither a pothole nor a sinkhole, is what happens when layers of asphalt fall away, exposing underneath layers of asphalt in which the road's foundation is scarred but not damaged as with a pothole. As these three types of blemishes expose, asphalt is a porous, temporary, unstable surface for roadways. Yet asphalt is ubiquitous in the paved terrain, with concrete, gravel, and dirt less often used on publicly-maintained roadways. The meaning of smooth pavement is a semiotic of society governed through law and order, as attention is devoted to the repair of potholes. When ignored, the otherwise smooth, straight, asphalted roads can result in anarchy.

Accelerationist Liminalities

This book has engaged with asphalted pavement as a site of legal materiality for considerations of legal geography moreso than driver-based auto-mobility. Yet, as a site paved for cars, travel itself, as the foundation for the field of automobility, is premised upon pavement. Travel can be characterized through rates of speed. While some paved terrains are constructed for slower speeds, others are built for acceleration. Nonetheless, the relationship between travel and pavement is based upon acceleration. While speed limits exist and law enforcement patrols the heavy-footed, the accelerationist liminalities of the roadscape animate further the socio-legal status quo in which normative rates of speed are framed through the different contexts of different roadscapes. For example, the car is no longer the preferred means of travel. In some locales of the United States, religious groups including the Amish or the Mennonites use only non-motorized forms of transportation, such as the horse and buggy.

In this way, the roadscape, as a paved public landscape, serves vehicular as well as equine forms of travel. In these paved environments, the horse is legally on equal footing with the rubber tire despite the decreased rate of speed. However, accidents and death ensue from cars that hit buggies, which stand little chance of surviving such a crash. Bicycles are a similar non-motorized form of transportation that share the roadscape with cars. The recent politicizing of reserved road space for bicycles ignored by motorists has resulted in the phenomenon of "bikelash" (Wild et al 2018). Bikelash is the reclaiming of asphalted space for bicycles beyond the designated lanes reserved for bikes. This designated space is a reminder that pavement serves both a vehicularized and non-vehicularized public. This public, as Virilio (2006, 51) notes, is affected by speed limits insofar as "just as for the laws on speed limits, we are talking about acts of government, in other words of the political control of the highway, aiming precisely at limiting the 'extraordinary power of assault' that motorization of the masses creates." In the zoom-scape (Schwarzer 2004), acceleration is framed through the conditions of the roadscape that might either merit speeding up or slowing down. With the possibility of striking a horse and buggy or bicycle with a moving car, the roadscape becomes a normative environment for morality that pits acceleration against the liminalities of context and presumptions of common sense. Given the recent rash of renegade motorists around the world who drive into crowds, outdoor markets, and holiday parades with the intent to drive over as many pedestrians as possible, the relationship between assault and a motorized weapon dangerously increases. The public space of the roadscape seems likely enough to maim its occupants in an accident involving two or more cars, but the act of driving the car into a non-vehicularized public gathering is vehicular terrorism. In U.S. Public Law No. 115–400, "Vehicular Terrorism Prevention Act of 2018," the Department of Homeland Security is responsible for providing emergency services to the "private sector," presumably referring to areas affected by acts of vehicular terrorism. Interestingly, the private sector of the vehicular environment as described by this law is what this book has termed the paved public landscape, or the roadscape.

As I conclude this chapter, Russia is assembling a 60km convoy of tanks on roadways to invade Ukraine and surround its capital, Kyiv, even as thousands of cars clog the roads out of the Ukraine in attempts to evacuate and flee the violence. In using the asphalted terrain for political violence, President Vladimir Putin of Russia is using the roadscape in a similar way to supporters of former U.S. President Donald Trump in the weeks prior to the contested presidential election of 2020. While driving down the road in Texas in late October 2020, supporters of Trump driving white vehicles surrounded the campaign bus of Joseph Biden/Kamala Harris in attempt to force it off the road. Known as the "Trump Train" (Shill 2020), convoys of Trump supporters drove down American highways intimidating drivers and stopping traffic on major interstate highways. Using the roadscape in pavementeering attempts to forge politics with violence and intimidation, a similar convoy of semi-truckers drove from the West Coast to Washington, D.C. in early March 2022 to protest the U.S. government's policies on vaccination and other policies in place to prevent the spread of Covid-19. Known as "the People's Convoy," the group encircled the nation's capital

Figure 3.3 Pavement Ends, Hawai'i Island

using the highway referred to as the Beltway, which wraps around the city (Dasgupta 2022). As an example of pavementality, the use of the car on pavement for purposes of physical violence catapults the roadscape into the realm of public terror that crosses unsaid boundaries that cars don't hit people. Furthermore, the assemblage of cars (or tanks) with drivers to travel collectively for purposes of violence propels the normative space of the roadscape as a site for travel with the accompanying accelerationist liminalities into spaces of lawlessness. To close, we can consider the roadscape through the lawscape as keenly articulated by Philippopoulos-Mihalopoulos (2015, 71) as "operat[ing] as a continuous manifold in which law and space emerge interfolded."

Notes

1 *Lyng v. Northwest Indian Cemetery Protective Association* 485 US 439 (1988).
2 *State ex rel. Kobayashi v. Zimring*, 566 P. 2d 725 (Haw. 1977).

Reference List

Allen, Kristen. 2017. "Forced To Build Hitler's Highways." *Handelsblatt Today*, January 21, 2017. Accessed March 11, 2022. www.handelsblatt.com/english/politics/forgotten-victims-forced-to-build-hitlers-highways/23565576.html.

Associated Press. 2018. "Fissure 8's Spatter Cone is as Tall as Aloha Tower." *Star Advertiser*, July 3, 2018. Accessed March 11, 2022. www.staradvertiser. com/2018/07/03/hawaii-news/fissure-8s-spatter-cone-is-as-tall-as-aloha-tower/.

———. 2019. "Mayor Kim Trying to Find Way Out of TMT Impasse with More Talk." *Hawaii Public Radio*, July 29, 2019. Accessed March 11, 2022. www. hawaiipublicradio.org/local-news/2019-07-29/mayor-kim-trying-to-find-way-out-of-tmt-impasse-with-more-talk.

Augé, Marc. 1995. *Non-Places: An Introduction to an Anthropology of Supermodernity*. Translated by John Howe. London: Verso.

Bennett, Jane. 2010. *Vibrant Matter: A Political Ecology of Things*. Durham, NC: Duke University Press.

Blomley, Nicholas. 2011. *Rights of Passage: Sidewalks and the Regulation of Public Flow*. New York: Routledge.

Brestovansky, Michael. 2020. "Leilani Estates Residents Divided about Road Up Fissure 8." *Hawaii Tribune Herald*, December 25, 2020. Accessed March 29, 2021. www. hawaiitribune-herald.com/2020/12/25/hawaii-news/leilani-estates-residents-divided-about-road-up-fissure-8/.

———. 2021. "DPW: No Road Permit Needed for Homemade Fissure 8 Route." *Hawaii Tribune-Herald*, January 3, 2021. Accessed March 11, 2022. www.west hawaiitoday.com/2021/01/03/hawaii-news/dpw-no-road-permit-needed/.

Brigham, John. 1990. *Property and the Politics of Entitlement*. Philadelphia: Temple University Press.

Dasgupta, Sonia. 2022. "Truck Convoy Hits the DC Beltway for the 4th Day, This Time with Sen. Ted Cruz." *WJLA ABC News*, March 10, 2022. Accessed March 11, 2022. https://wjla.com/news/local/truck-convoy-trucker-protest-peoples-convoy-dc-beltway-covid-19-vaccine-mandates-gas-prices-biden-trump.

De Certeau, Michel. 1984. *The Practice of Everyday Life*. Translated by Steven Rendall. Berkeley: University of California Press.

Delaney, David. 2010. *Nomospheric Investigations: The Spatial, The Legal, and the Pragmatics of World-Making*. New York: Routledge.

Goldman, Emma. 1933. "An Anarchist's Look at Life." Speech given on March 1, 1933 at Foyle's Twenty-Ninth Literary Luncheon in Grosvenor House, London.

Higgins, Andrew. 2020. "Along Russia's 'Road of Bones,' Relics of Suffering and Despair." *New York Times*, November 21, 2020. Accessed 11 March 2022. www. nytimes.com/2020/11/22/world/europe/russia-stalin-gulag-kolyma-magadan.html.

Hurley, Timothy. 2018. "Hawaii Supreme Court Rules in Favor of Building Thirty Meter Telescope." *Star Advertiser*, October 30, 2018. Accessed March 11, 2022. www.staradvertiser.com/2018/10/30/breaking-news/supreme-court-rules-in-favor-of-tmt/

Ingold, Tim. 2016. *Lines*. New York: Routledge.

Jones, Caleb. 2019. "Hardships from Hawaii Volcano Stretch on 1 Year Later." *Associated Press*, May 3, 2019. Accessed March 11, 2022. https://apnews. com/article/hawaii-north-america-us-news-ap-top-news-lifestyle-5b2fc2fc37a 445f9a5455de706794a66.

Khon2. 2016. "State Seeks Person of Interest After Rocks Found on Mauna Kea Road." *Khon2 News*, May 26, 2016. Accessed March 11, 2022. www.khon2.com/ local-news/state-seeks-person-of-interest-after-rocks-found-on-mauna-kea-road/.

Lauer, Nancy Cook. 2021. "Neighbors Seek Purchase of 'Fissure 8' with PONC Funds." *West Hawaii Today*, March 9, 2021. Accessed March 11, 2022. www.hawaiitribune-herald.com/2021/03/09/hawaii-news/neighbors-seek-purchase-of-fissure-8-with-ponc-funds/.

Lefebvre, Henri. 1991. *The Production of Space*. Translated by Donald Nicholson-Smith. Malden, MA: Blackwell.

Mauna Kea Science Reserve Master Plan. n.d. University of Hawai'i. Accessed March 11, 2022. https://web.archive.org/web/20090920101000/http:/www.hawaii.edu/maunakea/7_recreation.pdf.

Metcalfe, John. 2017. "Portland Anarchists Want to Fix Your Street's Potholes." *Bloomberg City Lab*, March 15, 2017. Accessed March 11, 2022. www.bloomberg.com/news/articles/2017-03-15/portland-anarchist-road-care-fixes-potholes-anonymously.

Ostrom, Elinor. 1990. *Governing the Commons: The Evolution of Institutions for Collective Action*. Cambridge: Cambridge University Press.

Philippopoulos-Mihalopoulos, Andreas. 2015. *Spatial Justice: Body, Lawscape, Atmosphere*. New York: Routledge.

Pili, Kamaka. 2021. "Fissure 8 Officially Given a Hawaiian Name." *Khon2 News*, March 4, 2021. Accessed March 11, 2022. www.khon2.com/local-news/fissure-8-officially-given-a-hawaiian-name/

Portland Bureau of Transportation (PBOT). n.d. "Pothole Sinkhole and Repair." Accessed March 11, 2022. www.portlandoregon.gov/transportation/article/319627#life.

Scheingold, Stuart. 2004. *The Politics of Rights: Lawyers, Public Policy, and Political Change*. 2nd ed. Ann Arbor, MI: University of Michigan Press.

Schwarzer, Mitchell. 2004. *Zoomscape: Architecture in Motion and Media*. New York: Princeton Architectural Press.

Shill, Gregory H. 2020. "How Vehicular Intimidation Became the Norm." *The Atlantic*, November 3, 2020. Accessed March 11, 2022. www.theatlantic.com/ideas/archive/2020/11/how-trump-train-trucks-became-a-political-weapon/616979/.

Valverde, Mariana. 2003. *Law's Dream of a Common Knowledge*. Princeton: Princeton University Press.

Virilio, Paul. 2006. *Speed and Politics: An Essay on Dromology*. Translated by Mark Polizzotti. Cambridge, MA: MIT Press.

Wild, Kirsty, Alistair Woodward, Adrian Field, and Alex Macmillian. 2018. "Beyond 'Bikelash': Engaging with Community Opposition to Cycle Lanes." *Mobilities* 13 (4). https://doi.org/10.1080/17450101.2017.1408950.

Index

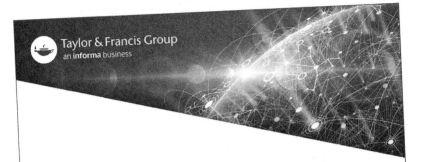

Printed in the United States
by Baker & Taylor Publisher Services